Musings of a Centenarian
or
Poetry Personified

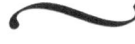

—————— Milton J. Ross ——————

iUniverse, Inc.
New York   Bloomington

Musings of a Centenarian or Poetry Personified

iUniverse books may be ordered through booksellers or by contacting:

iUniverse
1663 Liberty Drive
Bloomington, IN 47403
www.iuniverse.com
1-800-Authors (1-800-288-4677)

ISBN: 978-1-4401-7951-8 (pbk)
ISBN: 978-1-4401-7952-5 (ebook)

Printed in the United States of America

iUniverse rev. date: 10/12/09

DEDICATION

To our son, Dr. Robert D. Ross,

Without whose untiring efforts, support, and encouragement, this work would never have been accomplished.

And to my dear wife, Ann Ross, for her patience and forbearance as well as her encouragement during this period of conception and construction.

Forward

Now during my declining years, after passing the century mark I find myself deriving particular pleasure in creating these pearls of poetry.

I have enjoyed relating the experiences of the past hundred years such as biographical events, joyous holidays, natural phenomena, individual idiosyncrasies, Trowbridge trivia, and various other things that occur in a lengthy lifespan.

In the last two years, I have produced over a hundred examples of poetic feat.

I do hope that these verses will find a favorable response and prove both edifying and entertaining for those who are interested in this form of literature.

INTRODUCTION

Just prior to the celebration of my father's 100th birthday, he attended a poetry writing class at the retirement park where he and my mother live. For one of his first assignments he wrote his "Thoughts on Being 100 Years Old" and at his birthday party read this and another poem he had penned. I had the honor of emceeing the birthday celebration, and despite the presence of many older friends and relatives, no one had previously attended a birthday party for someone turning 100 years of age. Even today, I can still feel the warmth, glow and love in that room that day for my father. Even those people from the hotel working the party sensed the momentousness of that landmark occasion and worked extra hard to make the day unforgettable.

My father is a remarkable man and even today as he turns 102, looks and acts like a man many years younger. He continues his daily routine of an hour of exercises and stretching in the morning and twice daily pulls on his rowing machine of 100 strokes each. At the dinner table he continues to quote Chaucer and Shakespeare and remembers an incredible volume of family, social and political history.

My mother is no less incredible as she approaches her 96th birthday, and she should get a lot of credit for my father's longevity. While she moans that she still can't change him in the ways she would like, it is clear that their relationship has kept them both going strong as they continue to help and look out for each other.

As my father continued to write poems, I began to type them and print them out in a large font, so that he could read them aloud. He received very positive feedback when he did so, which in part spurred him on to continue this new hobby. I promised him when he had written 100 poems, I would help publish them in a book. Thus began a remarkable 2 years when each week when I would dine with them, the first thing I would be handed would be a new poem, frequently before the "Hellos" had even been said.

As the project progressed, I encouraged him to write about some of the events in his life with historical significance. He always talks about his love of horses and cars and can tell about each automobile he ever owned beginning with a used 1929 Ford Model A. Not only did these make for interesting subjects for his writing, but I used the list of cars he owned to create the centerpieces for the guest tables at his 100th celebration. Each table had a reproduction of one of these cars and each guest had a replica on their name cards.

My father takes great pleasure in reading his poetry, especially to the individual about whom the poem is about. He also loves it when the poems show up in the newsletter published at the residence where they live. He did write an autobiography when he turned 90, entitled "Max," which was copied and bound with the help of my uncle Albert Zack. I find it wonderful that he is making use of the skills from his younger days as an English teacher and drama director.

In putting together the photographs to accompany the poems, I found great illustrations from the family albums. I also used my favorite nature pictures taken over the years which Milton and Ann now enjoy in their apartment on that "new fangled" digital picture frame.

Working with my father on this project has given all of us the opportunity to relive a lot of his life and times and to share with him his favorite subjects of family, nature, and the people in his life. We are truly blessed to have my parents with us and in such condition to be able to enjoy each other and the gifts they give us. This collection of poems offers a wonderful insight on over a hundred years of living on this earth from a man whom I greatly love and admire. It is our hope that you will enjoy his works and his perspectives on this amazing world.

Robert D. Ross

Table of Contents

Part III: Nature

Part IV: People

Part V: School

Part VI: Trowbridge

Part VII: Miscellaneous

Part 1: Biographical

The Ross Family

In my family when I was growing up

There were just enough of us to fill an imaginary cup.

Besides my parents, there were of children three,

Two girls and one boy, and that boy was me.

My older sister and I were very much alike,

But the younger one was as different as different can be.

My older sister and I both became school teachers,

While my younger one followed other paths with quite different features.

During World War II, she served in the U.S. Army's Woman's Auxiliary Corps,

And after that she got married and two children she bore.

This is what happened to the original family of five,

And now I am the only one who is still alive.

Growing Up

In the years from 1915 to 1924

I practically grew up in a shoe store.

My family then lived in a "flat"

(an abode of that sort was called just that).

My father had a business selling shoes

So living above the store gave us nothing to lose.

In fact, it was very convenient for us

To have work place and home together with no fuss.

I learned how to be a salesman at an early age

Even though I was too young to earn any wage.

Later on while in high school I did work in downtown Detroit

Because by that time in the art of selling, I had become quite adroit.

At Wise Shoe Store on Woodward I sold women's shoes

And at Hanover Store, also on Woodward, I sold men's shoes.

On Saturdays this was my occupation

With nothing but good news

And that is what I did until I was ready for college

Where I did go in order to seek more knowledge.

One Summer Vacation

In 1923 there were three very popular summer resorts

That attracted people from Detroit of all sorts.

There were cruise ships of tremendous size

That would carry the visitors through friendly skies.

The "St. Clair" went to Tashmoo Park

The "Boblo" sailed to Bob-Lo Island on a happy lark.

Then there was the "Put-in-Bay" that went to the island of the same name

Where vacationers could disport themselves without shame.

I spent the whole summer there working as a hotel greeter and general factotum

Before I returned home to go back to school in the autumn.

At Put-in-Bay I enjoyed my visit and my work during my stay.

And now I also had the wherewithal to pay my way.

Put-In-Bay, Ohio

During my summer vacation in the year nineteen twenty three

When from school and study I was gleefully free.

I sought employment of some sort to occupy my time

And incidentally earn a stipend more than a dime.

I was fortunate to find a good friend who answered my need

He responded to me with both work and good deed.

He told me of an opening in a popular summer resort

Where he had spent the previous summer building a court.

I quickly applied for the job and was duly accepted

So there in Put-in-Bay I spent that summer at The Commodore Inn

Living a different kind of life and working my reward to win.

Nineteen Forty Three

In 1943 while World War II in Europe was being fought

Among many others, by the army draft I was caught.

It was during the month of January when I was 35

That many were leaving home hoping to come back alive.

Off to training camp we all did go

With spirits high, but feelings low.

Most of the draftees were youthful in age

Too young for anyone to be considered a sage.

I was almost like a father to them

But by the army not thought too old to ban.

In camp when my personnel file revealed

That I had experience in the teaching field

I was soon assigned to the clerical school

Where the trainees were selected from the army pool

To learn military correspondence and how to write morning reports

As well as typing, for preparing forms of all sorts.

And that's how I spent part of my army career

Before going on to duties much more severe.

Anniversary Song or Holy Matrimony

Some five and fifty years ago

I met a comely lass.

By her I was so beguiled I could not let her pass.

Indeed, soon afterward I joined with her in holy matrimony.

About this union of two single souls

There was nothing phony.

We two have lived, loved, procreated for more than a half century

And hopefully will continue until our lives are no more than just a memory.

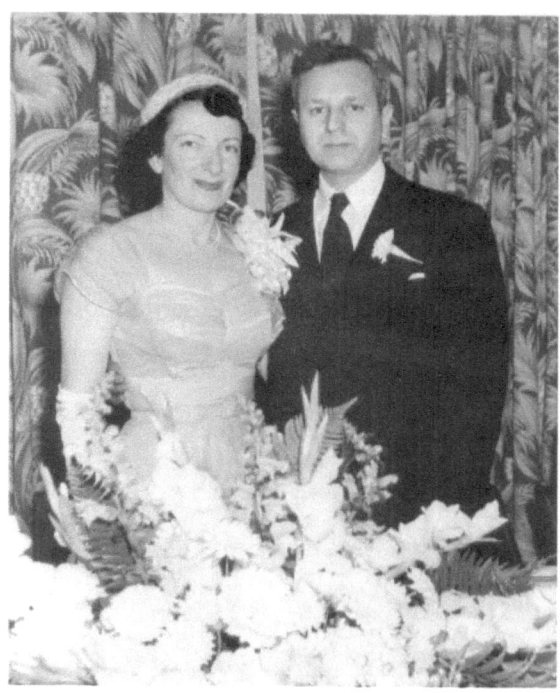

1953 Wedding of Ann and Milton

A Bit of Personal History

In the year 1915 – I was seven years old-

My family to Michigan did come.

Connecticut was the state we all did come from.

There, first in New Britain where I was born,

And then in Bristol

I spent the earliest years of what would turn out to be a long life.

And here in Detroit it was that I met the girl who was to become my wife.

Growing up on the east side of the city

I went to school there, both elementary and high.

Then to college to earn a B.A. and then an M.A.

All experiences that I look back on with nostalgia today.

My Family Tree-Part I

My mother and father were both born in Romania

Like almost everyone else they and their families wanted to come to America.

My father was born in 1877, my mother in 1881;

They never knew each other there, neither one.

They arrived in this country before the turn of the century

Each seeking a better life than in the old country.

They met through a relative on one side or the other

And married in 1903, both my father and my mother.

To them in 1905 was born a girl in the month of January.

That was my older sister, Malvern, who turned out to be both smart and pretty.

Then, almost two years later, in the month of September

I was born, and that was my family, as near as I remember.

But no, for on July 16th in 1914 another child came along,

My younger sister, Edith, was the last living offspring to belong

To our family of five who were now very much alive.

Of that group of people I am the only survivor.

Now I am over one hundred years old, and will continue more to strive for.

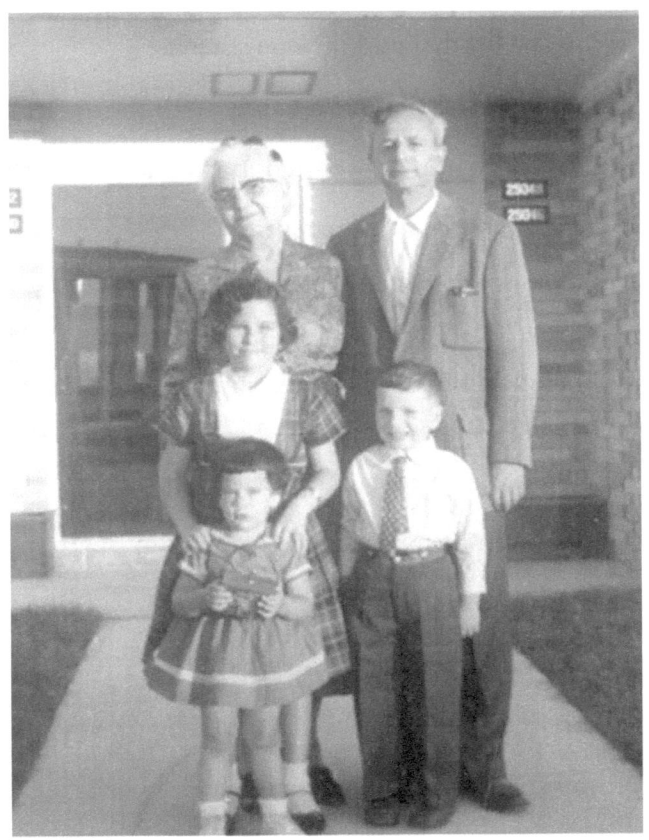

Grandma Caroline with her son and grandchildren
Karen, Julie and Rob

My Family Tree-Part II

In my mother's family there were seven sisters and one brother.

In my father's family there were five brothers and one sister.

Oddly enough, the one brother and the one sister

Found each other, married, and raised a family.

Another rather unusual event that occurred in my family's history

Was the union of my maternal grandparents.

When he was only seven years old my grandfather was forcibly taken by Russian army scouts

To Moscow and there schooled and brought up to be an officer in the Imperial Guard.

However, because of his desire to live the life of an observant Jew

At the age of twenty seven he managed to escape from the country.

Now a free man, he found his way to Romania

And there in a synagogue where he came to pray

He met my grandmother's father

Who in the spirit of friendship and religious beneficence

Invited the stranger to come to his home

And partake of the holiday celebration and feast.

That, I was told, was how he met and later married the young girl

Who was to become my grandmother.

(Note: Uncle Willie Rosenberg and Aunt Anna Berman)

Horses, Horses!

During summer vacations from college

Which I was attending seeking more knowledge

In 1926, 7, and 8, I went to camp at Fort Sheridan, Illinois

Where, at that time there was horse cavalry to my great joy.

I had always loved horses since I was a little boy,

And now I had the pleasure of riding nearly every day

Which to me was more important than any other kind of play.

The camp was a unit of the CMTC, or Citizens' Military Training Corps.

Of course, this was all back in the days of yore.

These were among the happiest days of my youth.

And I still relish the memories of that time, forsooth.

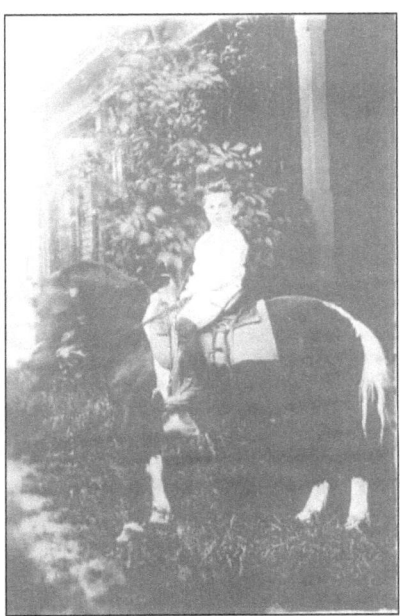

1912 Milt the Proud Horseman

How To Keep Fit

To keep physically and mentally fit

You have to give some time and thought to it.

Depending on your age and the condition you're in

If good health and a trim physique you desire to win

You need some form of exercise to pursue.

In my own case, at the age of a hundred and two

I can no longer walk several miles every day as I used to.

So I follow a program using my legs and my arms

With weights and my rowing machine to add to my (heh, heh,) charms.

By all these means I am daily involved

And thereby, find my physical and mental problems are mostly solved.

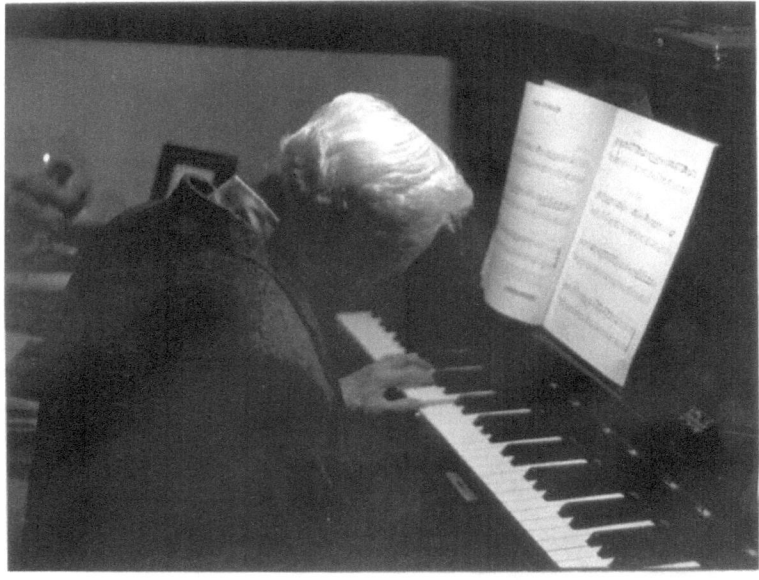

Author at the Keyboard

Recollections

My father, Joseph Rosenberg, was an orthodox Jew

Eight days after my birth, I was circumcised too.

As a family we observed all the major Jewish holidays.

In the spring of each year, there was always "Pesach" to be enjoyed

With its traditional foods and special ceremonies to be employed.

It was a celebration of the freedom from slavery by the Jews of the time

And now they would feel their lives could be sublime.

Then in the fall of the year there was always "Yontoivin" or the high holy days

To be celebrated in all the ancient ways.

First came "Rosh Hashanah" for the New Year,

And then "Yom Kippur" or the Day of Atonement

When you were supposed to fast, or not eat, to exculpate your sins of the past year.

These are among the memories of my youth and adolescence,

Fond recollections of my early life with my dearly beloved parents.

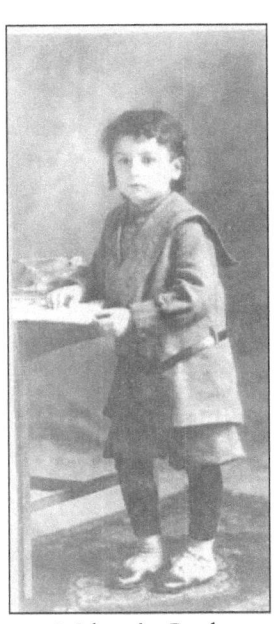

Milton's Curls

Family Roots

My mother was one of seven sisters and one brother.

All the children were taller than their mother.

That was probably because their father was a tall man.

He served in the military in Russia as an officer in the Imperial Guard.

At the age of thirty seven, wishing to live the life of a religious Jew,

He escaped from the country and found his way to Romania

Where he met my great, grandfather in a synagogue.

They became good friends, and he was invited to my relative's home for dinner.

There he met his friend's young daughter who later became his wife.

Eventually, along with other immigrants, they came to America

Where they found they could truly live the "American Dream."

Boy Meets Girl…and Wow!
Or How I Met My Wife

In October, 1945, I received my discharge from the U.S. army

At the conclusion of World War II.

I was now ready to resume my career and a normal civilian life.

At age 38, I was free, single, and carefree, with nary a worry nor a wife.

I was back home and at work, teaching high school English and directing school plays,

Just as I had been doing in my previous days.

Then I discovered a new activity

Which just happened to coincide with my own proclivity.

Our daily newspaper, The Detroit News, was sponsoring a hiking club

For people who liked to walk and talk.

By publishing a news column telling the time and meeting place

For all the units involved in their journalistic space.

So I joined a unit, and soon became a leader of my group,

And there is where I met Ann, my wife

With whom I want to spend all the rest of my life.

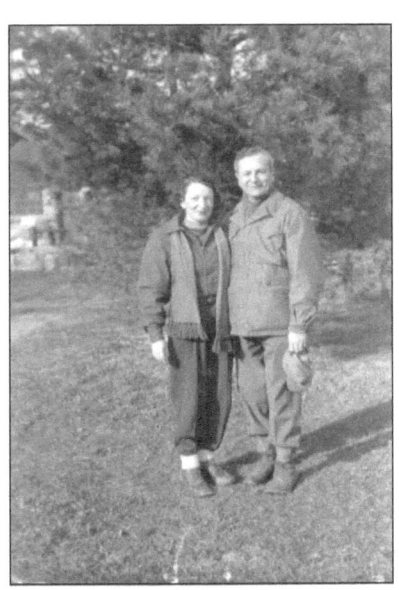

1953 Hikers Engaged

Thoughts on Being 100 Years Old

It's not easy being 100 years old.

That's a lot of years of living all told.

To complete a century here on earth

Filled with strife, struggle, tears and mirth.

Shakespeare spoke about the seven ages of man.

What seems at first a really lengthy span,

Becomes a brief moment of time for every man

Who is born, grows up, lives out his life.

Fortunate enough if he finds a good wife

With whom he can raise a family

And partake of the American dream.

It's not easy being 100 years old.

When I was fifty it seemed such a terrible event.

For me it was traumatic, and it definitely sent

Me into a state of depression and blues

From which fortunately I did recover, and now I choose

To welcome my fate and presently exult

In arriving at that celestial height

Where I now dwell both day and night.

As a centenarian who is thankful and grateful

For having been granted so many years

That I will continue my life with no more tears.

It's not easy being one hundred years old.

On Reaching a Hundred and One

Now that I have reached the age of a hundred and one

I find that life is not necessarily done.

My wife and I now know that living can still be a lot of fun

With each of us enjoying daily events,

Especially being with our only son

And daughter-in-law and grandson too.

Even though our family is limited to only a few

We are close, solicitous, loving and caring

With good vibes and relationships we are always bearing

The fruits of our labors and mutual sharing.

So take heart, all ye elderly seniors,

And remember, as that well known, former baseball player, Yogi Berra, was wont to say

"Life ain't over 'til it's over," come what may.

Finality

As I sit here in my room and look up at the sky so blue

I think of the many things I might still be able to do.

Since I am now on my way to one hundred and two.

Fairy tales, hobgoblins, leprechauns, and ghosts

Flit through my mind including hosts and hosts

Of people I have known and events I have witnessed

Over the span of a century and more.

Life on planet Earth has been good and very worthwhile.

Now I am preparing for my eventual departure.

And hoping to make my exit in very appropriate style.

One Hundred and Two

Now that I am one hundred and two

I find that there are things I can no longer do.

A daily walk for two miles or more

Is no longer possible for my legs so sore.

I now require the support of a walker or a cane

Because of weakness that makes me practically lame.

When it comes to dancing which I used to enjoy

That is out of the question for this old boy.

As for sex, forget it, that was something in the past

Although, hopefully, I was expecting it forever to last.

Heredity and Longevity

This poem was written at the suggestion of my good friend, Lucille Warren,

To whom my ramblings of the past few years have been anything but foreign.

She was as right as right can be

So here is the poem for all to see.

Perhaps because of my full head of hair and my fairly erect stance

I may appear younger than my years.

People are often surprised to hear I am 102 and now have no more fears.

Some have even asked to what I attribute my longevity.

My answer, half in jest, is that it is due to good heredity.

After all, my mother did live to be ninety five

Until then she was still very much alive.

Along with good heredity, there are some things that may help to prolong life.

Some of these are what is usually advised, like proper diet, no smoking, and regular exercise.

The last one is the one I wish to dwell on here

But I will be brief, dear reader, of that you may be sure,

Because I believe it has helped me the most, along with the use of the proper gear.

This involves a pair of dumbbells and a rowing machine,

And to use them daily I am ever so keen.

I also have other exercises involving the use of my legs and arms

And I perform them religiously, and without any harms.

All these activities done regularly and without fail

Help keep me in shape and also looking anything but frail.

Fruition

Of all the good things that have happened to me

Over the lengthy span of one hundred and three

Is my close knit family of five

Every one of whom is very much alive.

Consisting of wife, son, daughter-in-law and grandson.

Then, of course, there is also me.

It is always a pleasure when we get together

For holidays, birthdays, anniversaries and such

Always appreciated no matter the weather.

We do enjoy the presence of each other.

Our son, Robert, has achieved the goal of his dreams

To become a pediatric cardiologist, and then is seems

To get better and better because he is also a professor of medicine

At Wayne State University.

Robert's wife, Deborah, is also a professor.

She's in the Classics Department of the University of Michigan.

Therefore I feel my wife and I are blessed

To have such wonderful members of our family

And hope they continue to live in good health and prosperity.

We do love them all very much.

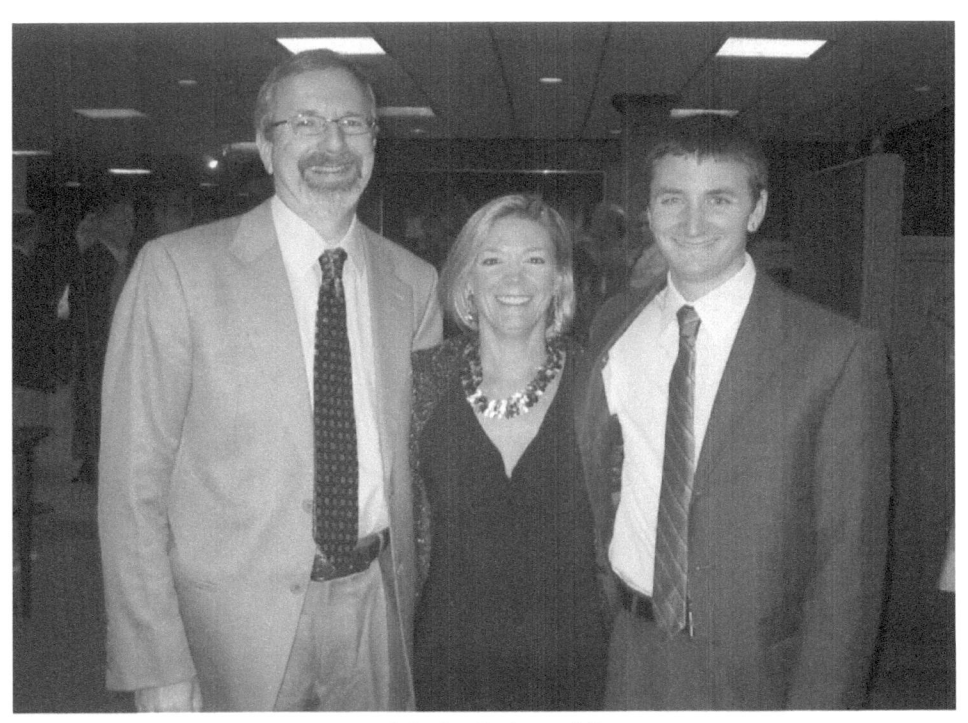

2006 Rob, Deb and Pete

Part II: Holidays

A Child's Delight

Tis the season to be jolly

Time for folks to hang the holly

Ol' St. Nick will soon be scrambling

down the chimney

of every home where dwells a little girl or boy

leaving for each child a much desired toy.

In the morning of the very next day

the children will awaken to find

all the gifts with which they hope to play.

Nothing is more fun than this,

The Christmas Day.

My First (and Only) Christmas Tree

Nearly a century ago when I was five or six years old

My family was living in a house on Franklin Street before it was to be sold.

This was in Connecticut in a small town called New Britain.

Where we had nary a pet, not a dog or a cat, not even a kitten.

But I had a very good friend about the same age who lived nearby

Whose father I thought was a really great guy.

I was a visitor in their home much of the time

As was my friend, often a guest in the home that was mine.

At his home one December day I saw his Christmas tree

With all the decorations, it was a wonderful sight to see.

I was so impressed by that beautiful sight

I rushed right home with all my might

To ask my parents why we couldn't have one too.

They told me that in our religion that was taboo.

Upon hearing this denial I cried, and then continued to be sad

Until something happened that was not at all bad.

In our house at that time we had a live-in immigrant Polish maid

Who performed her duties and was properly staid.

But out of her pity for me and out of the goodness of her heart

She did something that was quite far from being her part.

On her own she went out and purchased a small evergreen tree,

Put it up in my room and decorated it just for me.

That made me so happy I danced with glee.

And I have never forgotten that maid, nor my very own tree.

New Year's Eve

New Year's Eve at the Trowbridge on December 31, 2007

Was celebrated by food, drink, and dancing until almost eleven.

A professional dance team put on an exhibition

That drew from the crowd all their attention.

This was followed by the professionals

Drawing from the audience willing individuals

To cavort with them each in terpsichorean style

To each musical number enjoying all the while.

Those residents partaking in this joyful frolic

Mostly were Ann Ross, Betty Letwin, Edith Seutelberg, and Lew Cassel.

New Day-New Year

This morning the skies are all solemnly grey

As befits an unusually warm humid day.

The clouds hang heavily in the damp, humid air

And the day promises to be anything but fair.

Tis the day after Christmas and all through the land

People are planning for the year's last stand.

Soon a brand new year will be here

And we will all welcome it with jolly good cheer.

Always hoping the new will be better than the old

And bring joy and contentment for both the young and the elderly, all told.

Thanksgiving Day

Thanksgiving Holiday is a time for good cheer

Everyone enjoys it and it is an occasion without peer.

The family gets together at our son, Robert's house

Where they are warmly greeted by him and his spouse.

Debbie, his wife, cooks up a wonderful meal

And her sisters, Leslie and Tracy contribute to the big deal

By making all kinds of pies and other goodies

And Robert carves up the turkey to make it all real.

We dine sumptuously and eat to our heart's content

And finish the celebration with the time well spent.

Father's Day

In November of 1955, Robert David Ross arrived on the scene

A fact that under the circumstances was not so mean.

His father was 48 and his mother 41.

Not too old, but now their work was done.

No more offspring were to be added to the fold.

But the one we got turned out to be as good as gold.

Growing up, Robert attended Cranbrook Academy,

Then the University of Michigan and their medical school

With a summer at the Brompton Hospital in England

He interned at Northwestern University in Chicago

Then had a fellowship at the University of Cincinnati

Ending up at Children's Hospital of Michigan

As a pediatric cardiologist for more than 20 years so far

He continues to be a great son, a good husband, and a good father.

All this in addition to being in his religion a Cohane by birth.

Which in Hebrew mean the top order in the clan.

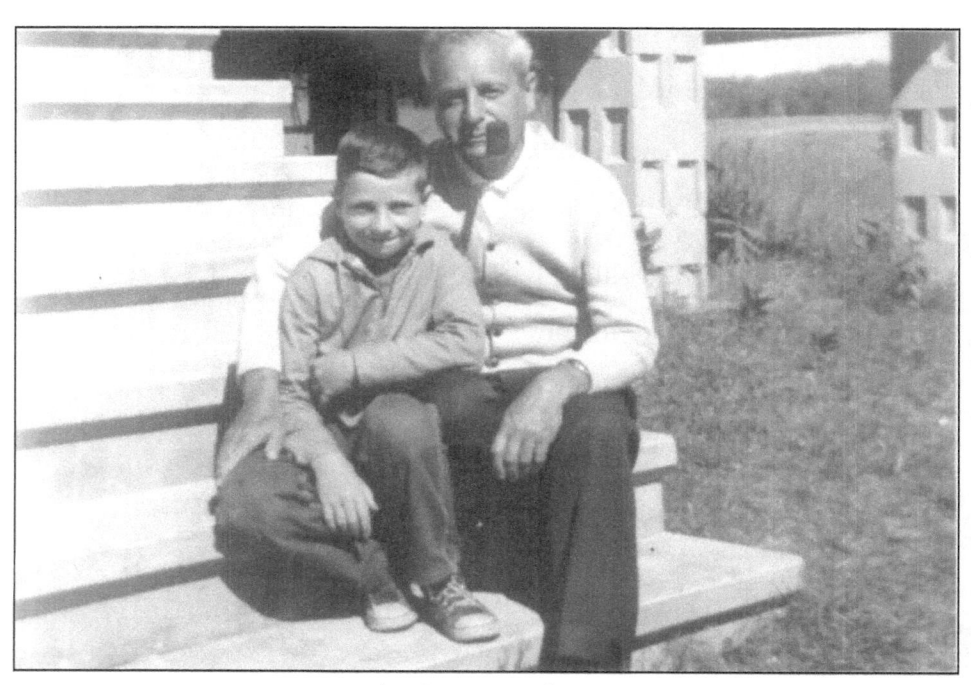

1963 Camp Michigania

New Year's Day

A brand new year has just arrived.

Now that it's January 1st in the year 2009

We all get older if not wiser with the passage of time

And need to achieve new heights of living and giving.

To do this we should strive to enhance the life of each individual

Who inhabits the environs of this terrestrial citadel.

All of us should look forward to greater improvement

In the lives of all who dwell on this continent.

Mother's Day

Mother's Day is celebrated each year

In the glorious month of May.

That rightly is considered to be a very important day

For without our moms, none of us would be here.

Besides, think of the care and devotion they lavish on their children.

A mother is not only necessary for the preservation of the human race,

She is also cherished by her offspring who will eventually take her place.

Thank God for all mothers who have made their contribution

Through all the years according to the "theory of evolution."

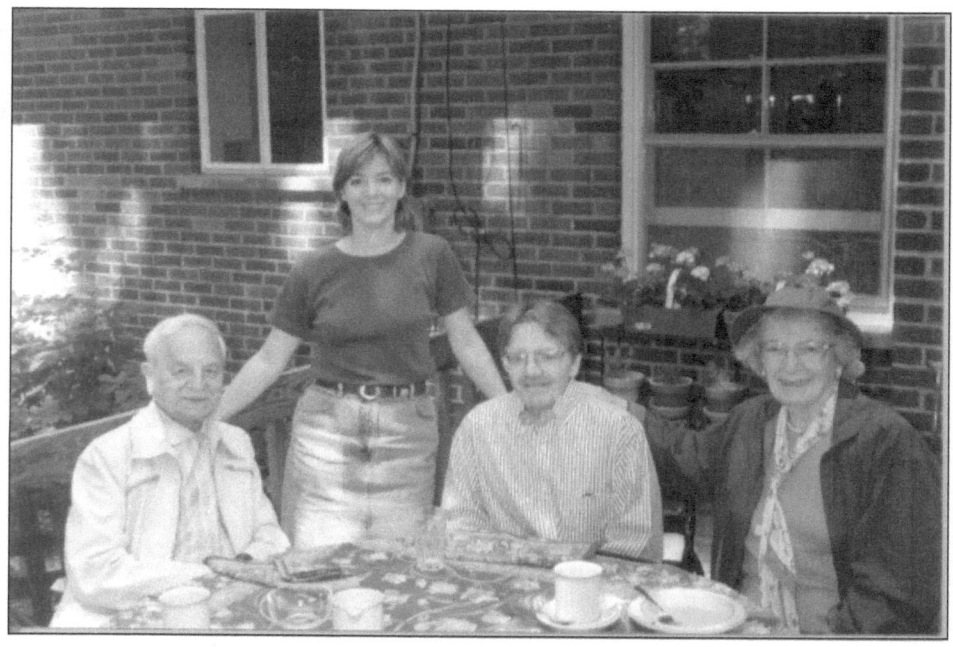

1995 Mothers Ann and Deb with Grandpas Milt and Art

Father's Day II

June 21st is notable especially for two things.

It marks the arrival of the summer solstice for one,

And the other event is Father's Day which it also brings.

Fathers should be appreciated for all that they do.

They provide support and protection for their children,

And also act as role models for them as they grow up to become young men and young women.

That is why we celebrate this day each year,

And that is also why for everyone with a father, it should be crystal clear.

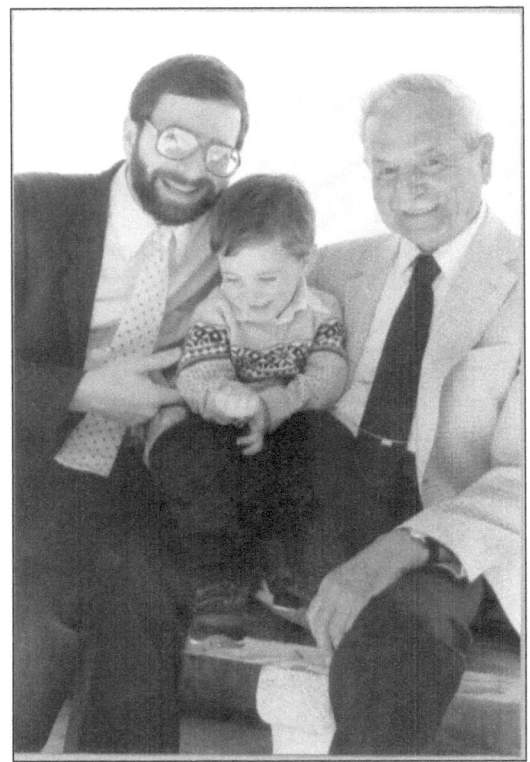

3 Generations of Ross Men

Part III: Nature

Dance of the Tree Leaves

(With apologies to the poet Joyce Kilmer)

Oft when at my desk I sit

Engaged in attempt to create a dramatic hit

To shape a phrase, I pause a bit.

And look up and out through my window pane

To see the trees that fill my view

And watch the leaves dance to and fro

Impelled by the gentle breezes that blow

From south to north or north to south.

And then these words come from out my mouth:

"I think that I shall never see

A thing as lovely as a tree."

And finally the poet, Joyce Kilmer,

Ends his poem with these lines:

"Poems are made by fools like me

But only God can make a tree."

Autumn 2007

The leaves on the trees are changing color, fall is here.

The weather is becoming cooler, winter is near.

Nature assures all's right with the world.

The seasons come and go, and the flag is unfurled.

Atop the buildings where it is wont to fly

From sunrise to sunset enlightening the sky.

And the musicians play all the tunes in their band

As the game of football reigns in the land.

BR-R-R
It's Cold Outside

Now that the leaves are falling off the trees

And winter approaches with its annual freeze.

The rain when it falls is cold, and it will soon start to snow.

The winds out of the north will begin to blow

And Jack Frost will be making his mark on each window pane.

We here in Michigan will again feel the same

As we do each year when the calendar denotes that December is here.

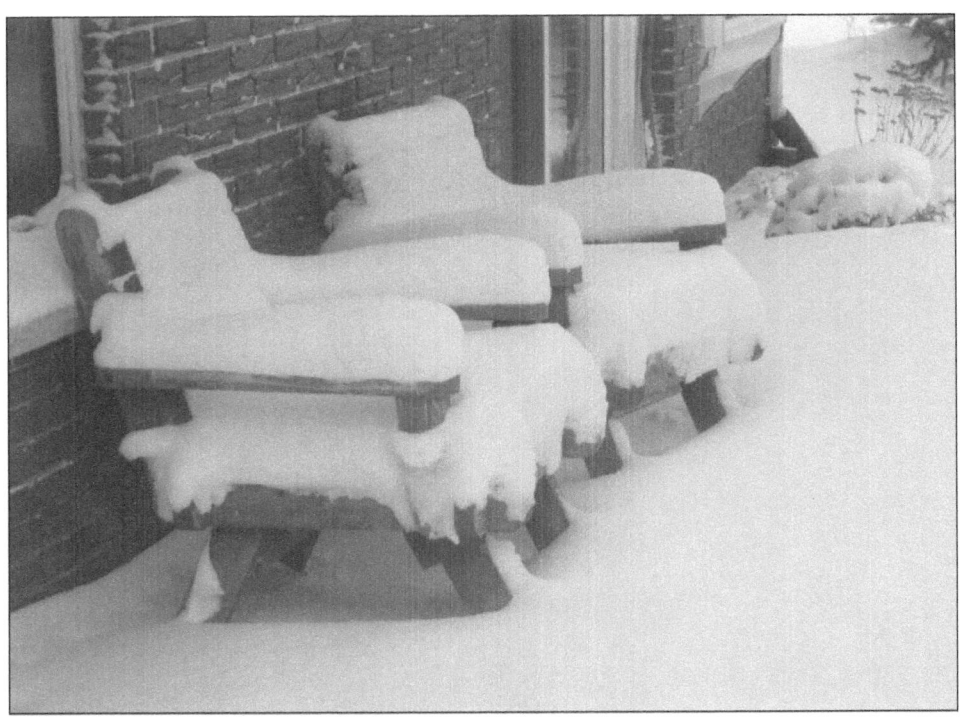

Transition

The trees outside my window

No longer have leaves, winter is here

The foliage is all gone, the limbs are all bare.

The denizens of the woods have departed.

There's not even the sign of a hare.

The snow flakes are falling,

Nature's frosting on the cake.

The birds are all gone to their home in the south

And now these words issue forth

From my mouth:

"If winter comes can spring be far behind?"

As someone once wrote in a poem, I find.

Clouds

As I sit by my window and gaze up at the sky

I se nothing that moves but birds that fly by

And then there are clouds that enter my view

As they move slowly across the heavenly blue.

Sometimes they form shapes that are interesting to watch

And sometimes seem almost low enough to reach out and touch.

Cumulus clouds for the most part they are

Floating gracefully and majestically in the distance so far.

In moments of meditation induced by this scene

I am overwhelmed by the increase in my senses so keen.

Regeneration

On December 21st winter officially is here

Marked on the calendar as the winter solstice this time of year.

Now the length of the day will slowly increase

And the darkness of night will continue as slowly to decrease.

In a gradual process the earth revolves 'round the sun

Before its annual journey is completely done.

When Spring finally arrives it will bring new hope

For all life to renew, so use water and soap

To wash away the old and welcome the new

Life goes on so all may enjoy it too.

Winter 2008

The ground is all covered with snow

The winds out of the north do strongly blow

The trees and the bushes are all covered in white

And all of the landscape is in much the same light.

Winter is here and will be for a while.

Warm clothing and heavy boots are now all in style.

Sniffles and coughs will soon fill the air

And people will suffer if they don't take care.

So take heed, one and all, be aware of the benefits you will reap

From proper nourishment, good habits and the proper amount of sleep!

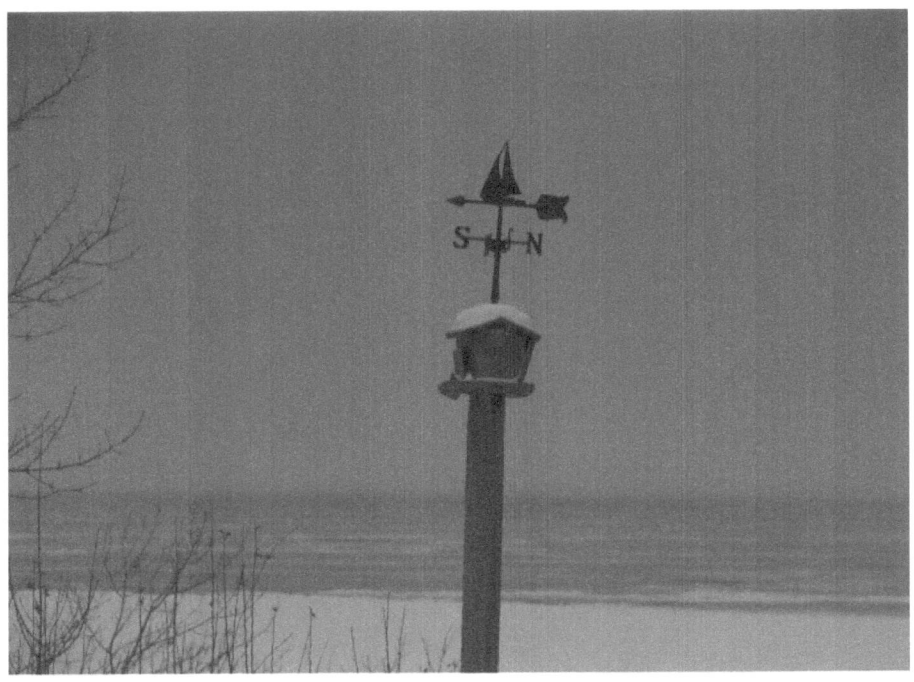

January 2008

The trees all heavily coated with snow

Stand ghostly white row upon row.

Winter is here for certain to stay

For several months more without delay

Picturesque it is without a doubt

But cold it is too with all Jack Frost' clout.

The children skating on the pond with cheeks aglow

Are delighted to play in the white, fluffy snow.

That is one of the things we have in Michigan to enjoy,

The change of season brings us happiness and joy.

The March of Time

Heigh ho! Spring is in the air.

The days are getting longer and they are mostly fair.

Warmer weather is on the way

And soon will come the merry month of May.

That will be followed by jumpin' June

With its promise (perhaps) of a full moon.

Shortly thereafter there will be July and August

With summer sports, picnics, and other fun

To be enjoyed by all who worship the sun.

And then the year will end with the final month of December.

Trees

Trees, I really appreciate them

I admire them, I love looking at them.

As I gaze out my bedroom window

I see nothing more, neither high nor low.

The thick cluster of arboreal beauty

Arouses in me feelings of peace, relaxation, and serenity.

Again I am reminded of Joyce Kilmer's famous lines,

"Poems are made by fools like me.

But only God can make a tree."

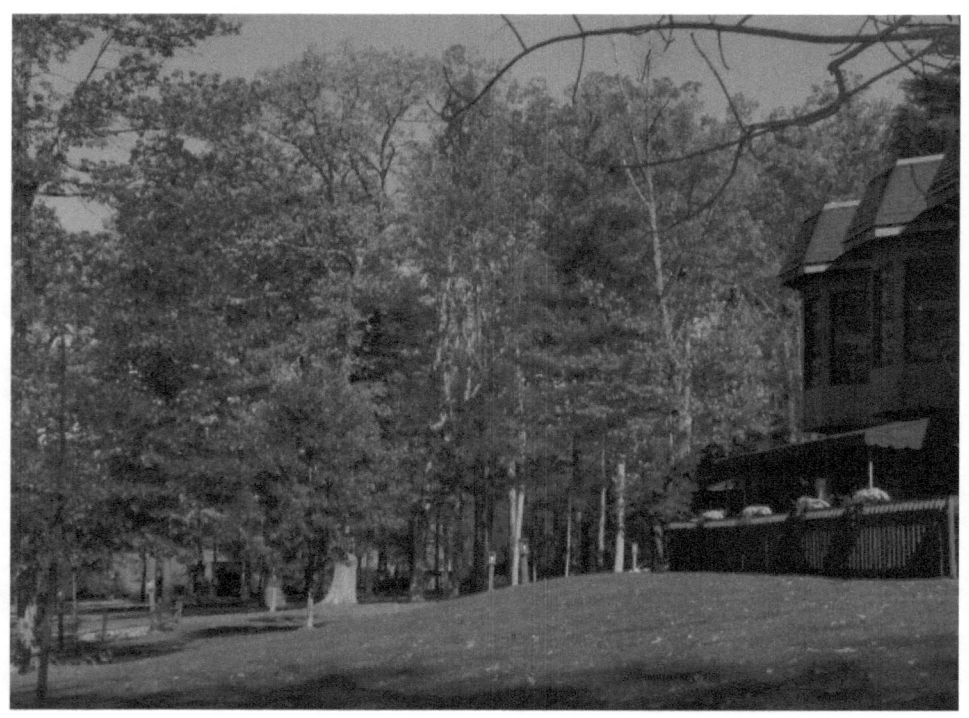

Summertime

It's June 20, and summer is officially here.

The weather's warm, it's time for a cold beer.

The sun is shining, the tree leaves are dancing in the breeze.

It will be a long time until we get the next freeze.

Baseball, soccer and tennis are all sports we may now enjoy

As spectators or participants we feel like, "Oh boy."

We should take advantage of all the fun the season affords

For all too soon summer will come to an end with all its rewards.

Cloud Formations

I am constantly intrigued by my view of the sky

With its patterns of clouds as they slowly go floating by.

Sometimes in individual blobs of fleecy white

Sometimes in banks as black as the night.

To me they portray in their different shapes

Images of animals and humans conjured up in my imagination

Providing me with subjects for my ardent admiration.

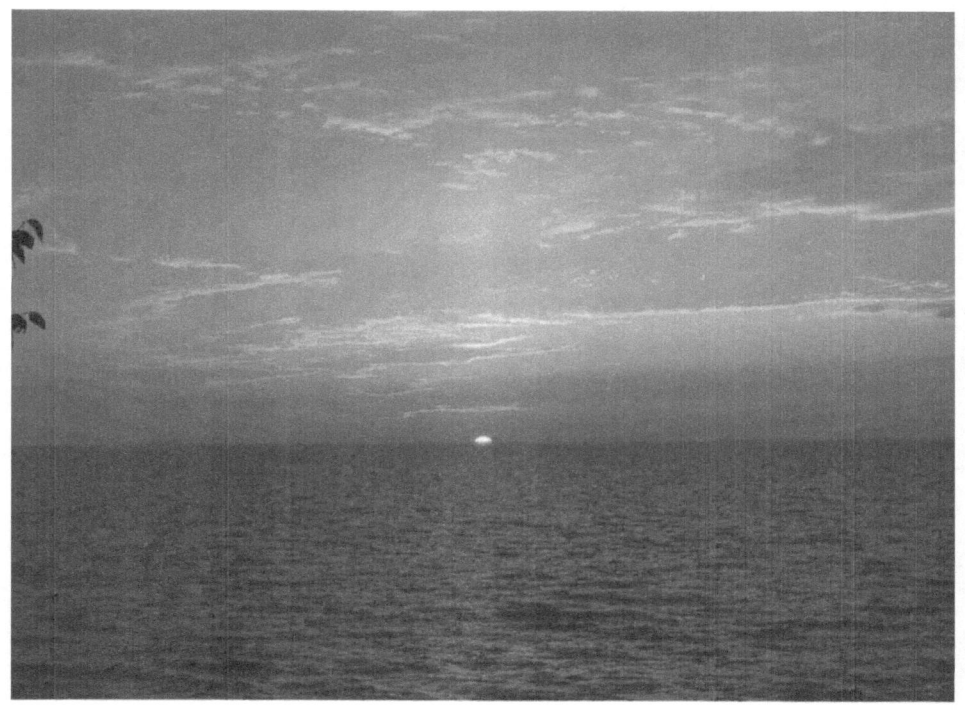

Fall

The autumn of the year is here again

The trees are losing their foliage

It is getting cooler and cooler

Summer is no longer of the weather the ruler

The days are getting shorter and shorter

The nights are becoming longer and longer.

Here in the Midwest to cope with the changes

We must needs to be stronger and stronger.

However we do enjoy the differing seasons

And for all of us there are various reasons.

Variety of climate can be very stimulating

It produces the proper atmosphere for serious celebrating!

The Change of Seasons

There is no sun at all on this November day

Clouds completely fill the sky

To see the sun today there is no way.

This morning there was a light snowfall

Now the snow is gone, but over the earth there is a pall.

Summer is long gone and fall is nearing its end.

With winter in the offing, and soon to be here

With all the cold, the snow, and foul weather we do fear.

Winter sports can be a pleasure for the young and strong

But for the weak and the aged the season is all wrong.

However, we can all enjoy nature's diversity

And benefit from the various kinds of activity.

Winter Solstice

It's December 21st and the winter solstice is here.

That means colder weather is getting very near.

There will be falling snow, howling winds, and icy streets

Which will require caution and care while performing driving feats.

Winter sports for the young and able now take over

While for the aged and feeble it means just seeking for cover.

Brisk walking, ice hockey, and sliding down hills

Are activities for those who are out looking for thrills.

While those folks too old or too weak for this kind of life to activate

Sit at home and contemplate how once upon a time they too were able to participate.

Spring Time

It is March 21st and Spring is here.

This day is also called the spring equinox

Meaning equal days and equal nights.

It marks the beginning of the loveliest time of the year.

It also marks the 56th anniversary of the marriage of Milton and Ann Ross.

That is over half a century of wedded bliss.

Our hope now is to continue our joy and love for the rest of our days.

"April Showers Bring May Flowers"

When Geoffrey Chaucer, the English poet who was purported to be

the father of the English language,

Produced the well known "Canterbury Tales" circa 1400,

He wrote at the very beginning of the "Prologue"

These lines that were written in Middle English:

"Whan that Aprille with his shoures sote

the drought of Marche hath perced to the roote,

And bathed every reyne in swich licour,

Of which vertu engendred is the flour..."

He was saying that the month of April with its frequent showers

Caused a renewal of life, and things began to grow again.

The effect it had on people was to arouse their feeling of hope and adventure

And they wanted to get out in the open and do some traveling and exploring.

That led directly to the journey and the story telling in "The Canterbury Tales."

Nature's Delight

As I sit in my room and gaze out through my window wide

I see some of the beauty of nature that is just outside.

There is a stanch of trees now fully covered

With a cloak of dark green leaves.

The foliage is so thick that nothing can be seen beyond it

Making a mask of verdure which for me is a great big hit.

Then there is the sky above, often dotted with fluffy white clouds

That look like giant pillows in the sky.

Sometimes those clouds can turn to an ominous looking black

Signifying the approach of impending storms.

When the weather permits I watch the sun setting in the West,

And that of all the sun's daily movements is perhaps the best.

This picturesque display of heavenly activities

Is only one example of nature's endless variety,

All these spectacles I am happy to behold,

And they can be witnessed by everyone whether young or old.

A Pink Cloud

Did you ever see a pink cloud?

Well, I did, and it was quite a sight to see.

It was a thing of beauty, and it was very good for me.

On this summer day, it was late in the afternoon

And the sun would be setting very soon

When the cloud was colored pink, like a blushing bride

While reflecting the dying rays of the setting sun

And this day was nearly over, with it diurnal duty done.

Part IV: People

ANN

My wife, Ann, has been for nearly fifty-five years

My constant companion and helpmate with no peers.

She is always there when I need her

And arguments between us truly are rare.

For a husband and wife to live without strife

Makes for a grand and remarkably beneficent life.

We have traveled together to many foreign lands

And never found time to be idle, on our hands.

Now in our declining years we hope to remain together

Until the time comes when we will be at the end of our tether.

Our Son, the Doctor

Our son, Robert, who is now fifty-two

Has always been able to thrive and make do

While advancing through the grades, college, and medical school

And at the same time abiding by the golden rule.

He is now a physician at Children's Hospital of Michigan

And also is in charge of the fellows who are working to begin

Their careers in Pediatric Cardiology

And therefore require a knowledge of the technology.

After twenty years and more in the service of children in need

He still carries on with his work as a really good deed.

And will continue with his healing practice in the future, take heed.

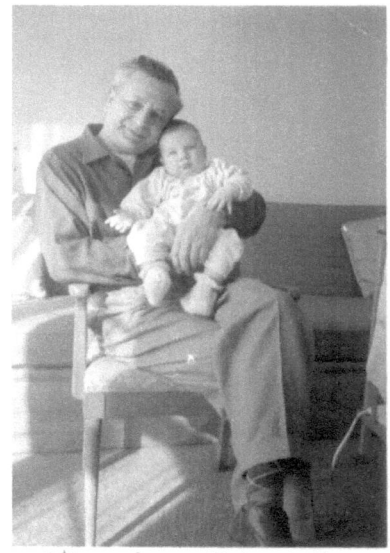

3½ mths.   Feb. 1956

Future Doc

Vera Rollin Burke

I have known Vera Rollin Burke

Since she was a comely lass of eighteen.

Even then, she exhibited a love of life so keen.

Then she married Bernard Rollin, a good friend of mine

And together they lived a full life so fine.

Bringing up two daughters, Wendy and Kathy

Who are now mourning their mother's demise.

Now all who knew her would be well advised

To participate in condolences for Vera, who now in her grave lies.

"Pax Vobiscum"

Rob's Birthday

Robert Ross is all of fifty-three years old

His arrival in the fall of '55 makes that all told.

He has now been at Children's Hospital for more than twenty years

As a pediatric cardiologist working along with his peers.

Not only does he continue to practice with great execution

But he also has other duties requiring a solution.

He teaches students at Wayne State University Medical School

And is in charge of the "Fellows" who are working by the clinical rule.

Then too he leads a group of doctors and nurses who go each year to an island in the Caribbean

Where they use their expertise to cure the diseases of children.

All of these activities keep Robert pretty well occupied

And to his career and personal fulfillment this is all tied.

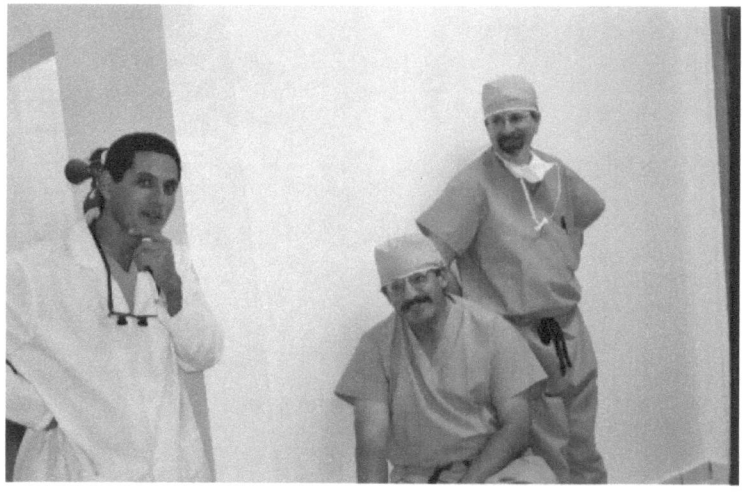

Docs in the Dominican Republic

Deborah Pennell Ross

The wife of my son with her siblings four

Two sisters and two brothers, and no one more.

Is a professor at the University of Michigan

Where she teaches Latin to those who wish to begin

A career of teaching the language of Julius Caesar in ancient Rome

Where his legions were famous from far and near to his home.

Besides her academic success, Debbie is a gourmet cook.

The dishes she prepares cause her guests no farther to look

For gastronomic delight-she is unparalleled in my book.

Peter Ross

My grandson, Peter, a scholar of French

Is more than a man, he is really a "Mensch."

Which in Yiddush means a person of great merit.

In high school he played tennis

And to other school teams he was truly a menace.

Now he continues the game to play

And may win a championship yet some day.

He is still in college although almost through

And then will embark on a career, hopefully too.

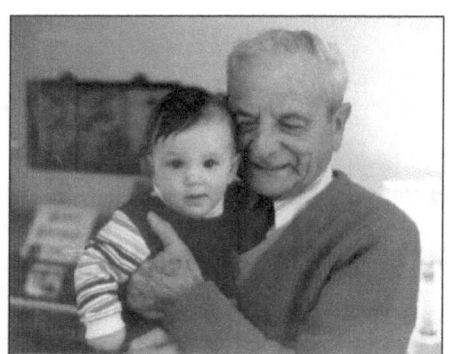 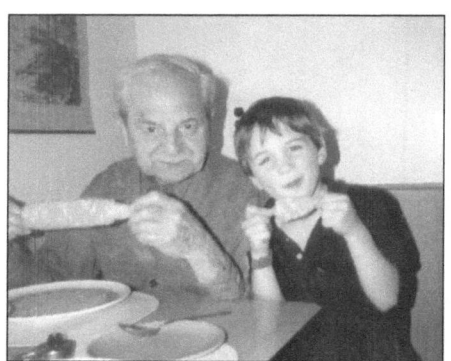

1984 Proud Grandpa   1988 "Corny Guys"

Ann Zack Ross

My wife, Ann Ross has now reached the age of ninety-five

Despite her advanced years, she is still very much alive.

She has always loved and still does love to dance,

And fortunately is still spry enough to take that chance.

She also loves to socialize with relatives and friends

And can be found doing just that at times without any ends.

In her younger days she was a teacher of some renown

Daily greeting her pupils and teaching them with nary a frown.

Now she is the mother of a son who is a pediatric cardiologist

And has a grandson who is about to graduate from college as a linguist,

Following in his mother, Debbie's footsteps.

To say nothing of being a good wife to her husband.

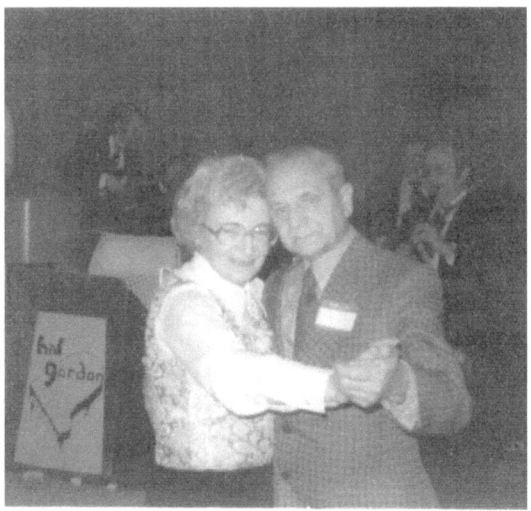

Ann and Milt celebrate their 25th Anniversary

Relatives and Friends

Albert Zack and his wife Ruth, close relatives, are leading a good life.

He, a good husband and father, she a good mother and wife.

Both are retired and enjoying the fruits of their labors

And are now and have always been very good neighbors.

Al, a former school principal, Ruth, a former school librarian,

Sometimes play Bridge with my wife, his sister and me, a centenarian.

Al is really a "gita n'shuma," Yiddush for a "good soul"

Helping his sisters and others while assuming the role

Of friend, relative and able advisor

To make all concerned ultimately the wiser.

Birthdays, anniversaries, some holidays we celebrate together.

This we do no matter the weather.

Friends and relatives should always keep in close touch

For life to be fully lived and enjoyed ever so much.

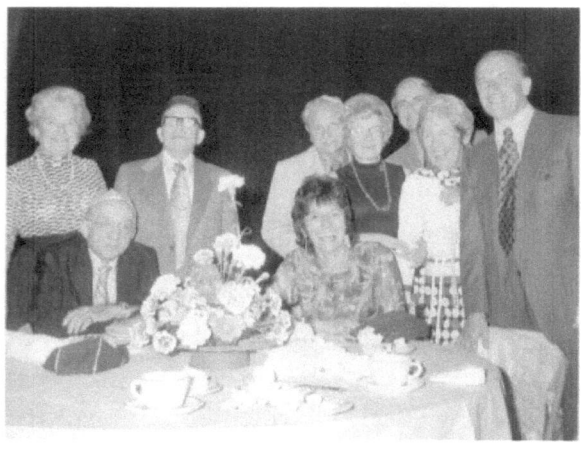

The Three Joes

The year was 1915, and in the Detroit area there were three men I knew named Joe.

My mother and two of her sisters were married to them so each had her own beau.

There was Joe Blau, Joe Rosenberg and Joe Shanbrom

The wives were Dora Blau, Caroline Rosenberg, and Sarah Shanbrom.

These three couples were not only relatives, but they were good friends as well.

They saw each other often, their relationship clear as a bell.

I remember all this because Caroline and her Joe

Were my dear father and mother.

For children they had me and my two sisters, but no brother.

All of us, parents, uncles, aunts, and their children

Were close and truly at that time members of the brethren.

Sarah Zack Levin

Sarah Zack Levin's birthday on the 23rd of March is today.

She has two sons, one for short, named Ray.

He is older, David is the younger.

There is a very close bond between brother and brother.

In her younger days Sarah was a teacher in the Detroit public schools.

Literature was her specialty, following all the rules.

She pursued her career with great diligence

Until matrimony intervened with all its pleasant sentiments.

She was happily married to Dr. Michael M. Levin

And ever since has been known as Mrs. Sarah Levin.

Hegira or Flight to a New Life

My wife's brother, Edward Zack, and his wife, Ruth Chereznia Zack

Did leave the Detroit area and move to Florida some years back.

Their two daughters, Nadine and Betsy, followed soon after

Now they lead happy lives, full of fun and laughter.

Both girls have husbands and two children each

Aaron and Benjamin for Nadine and Dr. Dennis Feldman

And Andrea and Samuel for Betsy and Dr. Abe Marcadis.

Grandparents Eddie and Ruth now are living in a senior residence

Happily ensconced and enjoying peace and benevolence.

The Missing Birthday

Many years ago when I was a mere broth of a lad

I posed a question to my mom and my dad.

When was I born, I wanted to know,

When was my actual birthday?

This was before the time when to school I would go.

That was in an era when birthdays were not such a big deal

Sure, they were celebrated, but not with such zeal.

By my mother and my father I was told

Briefly and somewhat vaguely, "it was on "Auf Yontoivin"

Which in Yiddush means around the High Holy Days.

Since these usually occur in early September

Somehow the sixth of that month became the date I remember.

I grew up believing that was my natal day

And I observed it each year all along the way.

However, when as an adult I required a passport to travel abroad

I sent a request for my birth certificate to Connecticut where I was born.

Not wishing any longer to remain so forlorn.

When to my surprise, I discovered that my birth occurred not on the sixth but on the ninth.

Even though the difference is small, the new certificate reveals

My "younger age," and that is as good as it feels.

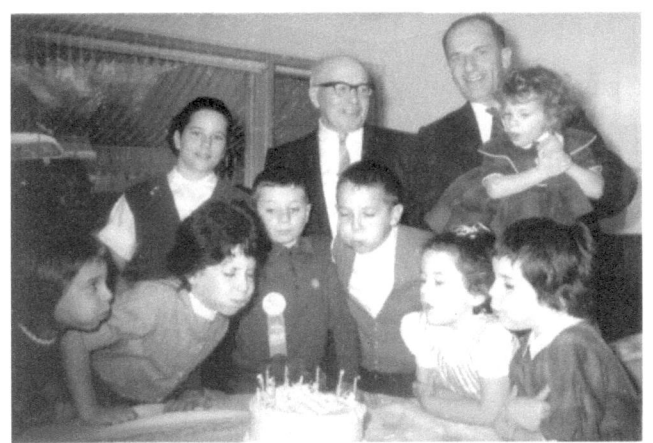

1962 Birthday with the Cousins

Ray Levin

Ray Levin, now that you are sixty four

You should continue on and strive to do more and more

To make the world a better place to live in

As your father did before you, Michael Levin.

He was a doctor who healed almost everyone he knew.

To emulate him you can do your share too

By setting an example for all to follow

And by doing good deeds and by service to humanity

Thus carrying on the Levin tradition

And filling out in life your foreordained mission.

Betty Letwin

Betty Letwin's birthday is today.

Of her presence in our midst we can truly say

That she brightens our lives with her easy smile and her dainty way.

We look forward each day to seeing her in the dining room

Where she can dispel any thoughts or feelings of despair or gloom.

Her appearance on the scene cheers us up for the rest of the day

And makes everything seem brighter than the merry month of May.

Esther Applebaum (ne Esther Ryback)

Nearly seventy years ago when I was working at the High School of Commerce

Where I was teaching courses involving grammar, literature, and interesting verse,

There was a young girl named Esther Ryback in one of my classes

Which were occupied by a bevy of comely adolescent lasses

Who were there primarily to study for secretarial jobs.

Their interests were mostly in bookkeeping, typing, and shorthand

But they were required to take English as well

And that's where I came in.

I mention Esther in particular because she is not only a former student

But has become a loyal and true friend

Who remembers all my birthdays and anniversaries

And never forgets that time of her youth

When she had a teacher whom she still calls "Mr. Ross."

Franca

My regular barber is a lady.

She is also a fine beauty operator.

She has both male and female customers.

She will cut your hair or curl your locks.

She also wears the prettiest frocks.

While clipping and fluffing the hair of her female clients

She maintains an aura of anything but silence.

She has a mother who lives across the sea in Italy.

As a loving and dutiful daughter she visits her twice a year,

Traveling all that long way with nary a fear.

I think that's a wonderful thing to do

And it is something she never will rue.

Franca's Beauty and Barbershop

Whenever I visit Franca's Beauty and Barbershop

I see her working until she is ready to drop.

She strives to make her female customers look like goddesses

And her male clientele like the picture of Adonis himself.

She cuts the ladies hair and shapes it into a perfect coiffure.

So if you want to look your very best

Go to Franca's and she will do the rest.

Gladys Bernstein

Gladys Bernstein of "The Park at Trowbridge" is a longtime resident.

She is also of the facility Council the esteemed president.

Then too she is in charge of the large library here

Where she catalogues the books and shelves them from front to rear.

Besides all this, she is a member of the group of play-reading actors

Which adds up to all the other different factors.

All these activities plus others make her a very much appreciated individual

By those who live here and occupy this special citadel.

Adrienne

There is a lovely lady who sits at our table in the dining room every day.

Adrienne is her name and she is quite a stately dame.

She helps make our meals interesting in every way.

Adrienne is the mother of four children, two boys and two girls

All of them are surely her joy and pearls.

One daughter lives in this area and she sees her quite often

When they go out to dinner or to a movie.

The whole family gets together when they periodically meet in the state of Vermont

In fact, that's where she is right now

Enjoying the winter sports and the glories of the State enow!

Henry Ford

Back in time almost a century ago

When life was lived at a pace that was relatively slow

A man by the name of Henry Ford

Was busy tinkering in his greasy shop

Until he developed a practical engine

And then installed it in a vehicle based on a horse drawn carriage.

Now he had what came to be called an automobile

Because it could move on its own without a horse to pull it.

By the year 1915, Henry Ford had a thriving factory in Highland Park, Michigan

Where he was turning out Ford cars almost as fast as water running out of a faucet

Thereby contributing to an era that came to be known as "The Industrial Age."

Fanny Andrews

Fannie Andrews works for H & R Block.

As my tax preparer she is steady as a rock.

She is steadfast and trustworthy,

And she looks good too.

So we get along fine together

Out of the blue.

I provide all the necessary facts

So for information she never lacks.

She does a businesslike job

So her I have selected

To perform the services for which

She has been elected.

Mostly About Harvey

At dinner at the Park at Trowbridge at table number twelve, we are four.

At this table there is little room for more.

Sitting on the East side is Harvey,

Ann is on the South, and Adrienne is on the North.

That leaves only me, and I am sitting on the West side, with my back to the window.

From that position, I can see everyone in from of me.

One of the things I noticed is that Harvey seems very fond of the ladies.

He likes to hold the hand of any lady that he knows.

Harvey knows a lot of people because he talks to everyone,

And that is how a lot of things are done.

Harvey has been married twice and he may be interested in finding a third.

But for that idea you have only my word.

Ann and Adrienne seem to enjoy conversing with him throughout the evening meal.

And that about brings me to the end of this interesting tale.

David Levin

As a son, David Levin is A-Number One.

For his mother Sarah, his love and devotion are never done.

Every night he calls her on the telephone

So that she never has the feeling of being left alone.

Their relationship of mother and son is eminently ideal

And their feeling of closeness is very real.

David and his wife Nancy have taken Sarah with them

When they have gone on trips to northern Michigan.

It is reassuring for all to see such behavior of an offspring to a parent

Revealing good and proper expression of sincere sentiment.

Julie and Dave

My niece Julie and her husband Dave are here visiting family and friends.

They don't come here often, but when they do they make amends.

They live in California and that is a long way from here.

They are our welcome guests and bring us good cheer.

Julie is an effervescent, ebullient talker and has a sparkling personality.

It is a pleasure to listen to her with nary a hint of banality.

Dave is one macho guy-there is almost nothing he cannot do.

He can fix anything that is broken,

Of his skill and ability this is just a token.

Together, Julie and Dave are quite a pair,

And we are their admiring relatives who for them do greatly care.

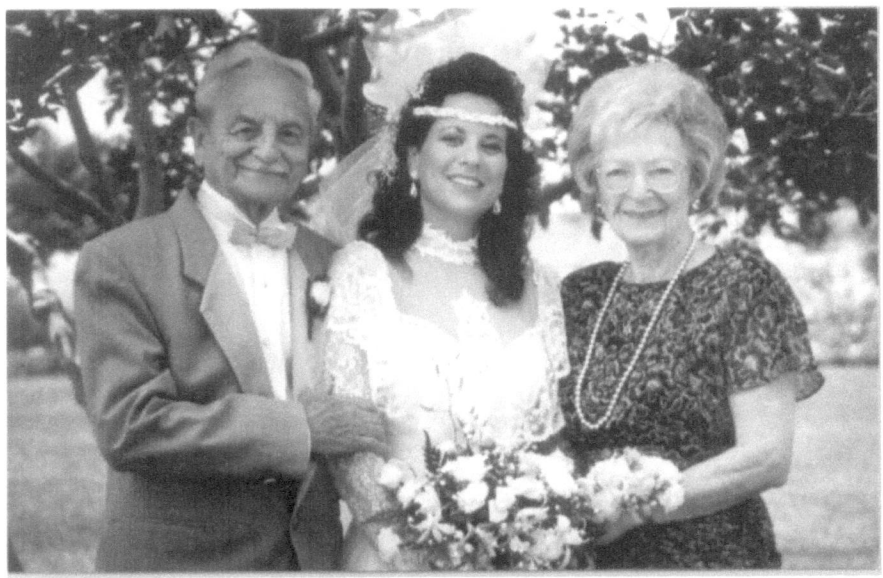

1988 Niece Julie's Wedding

Part V: School

This Poem Might Have Snob Appeal. In Fact It Might Be Called: "A Treat For the Elite." I Call It: "Pedagogy," A Poem For the Erudite

Acuity, atrophy, and attrition

Are examples of words sometimes used in the classroom

By teachers whose aim is not to confuse

But rather to encourage the student the dictionary to use.

Stimulating thought and clarity of expression

Often requires language of a higher dimension

And the student learns to employ the tools of his trade

So that the goals of his life can more easily be made.

School Daze

In 1924 when I was sixteen years of age

I finished high school considered something of a sage.

That was because I was placed in a pre-college program perforce

Including the four year study of Latin, of course,

Then thought to be suited only for those of superior intelligence

But now considered for anyone at all of normal good sense

So I did go to college

In search of more knowledge

And ended up in a career as a practicing pedagogue.

School's Out

During summer vacation in the year nineteen twenty three

When from school and study I was gleefully free

While seeking employment of some sort to occupy my time

And incidentally to earn a stipend more than a dime

I was fortunate to find a friend who came to my need

And responded in kind with work and good deed.

He told me of an opening in a popular resort

Where he had worked the previous summer building a court.

There is where I spent that summer at the Commodore Inn

Living and working there my wages to win.

Reminiscence

When I was a student in college

There to acquire something of formal knowledge

And incidentally to earn a degree

(It was then for only a nominal fee)

I discovered that not all learning

Comes from books and scholarly courses.

Many things are inculcated in the

Neophyte's mind in their very own houses.

To say nothing of those that meet in the street.

And there to acquire many of the facts of life

Completed by the acquisition of a very good wife

To have a full and rewarding existence

In this world of ours to wit and whence

Come all good things for those who have enough sense

To comprehend the teachings of school and experience.

Career Changes

In 1930 our nation was in the midst of a great depression

The economy was so bad that I hesitate even it to mention.

That year I finished college with a degree of B.A.

The next year was spent at the University of Wisconsin and earned me an M.A.

But things were still no better and a job was not available

So then to Teachers College I did go

Thinking I would continue to study some more

And by working hard managing to go along with the flow.

In 1932 I received my teaching certificate

And was ready to go to work.

But again with disappointment I was met....

Finally four years later the economy improved

And now I did get a job teaching and was moved

To start a career as a teacher of English and director of school plays

And did that for a while, but fate ordained otherwise.

My life now took a new turn

With the advent of war new lessons I was obliged to learn

The draft was on and in 1943 a soldier I became

One of my duties there was something of the same

For teaching military correspondence was part of the game.

Back in civilian life I taught some more

And then came the last change to even the score.

The business world offered an opportunity to advance

And in this field I progressed and took my last chance.

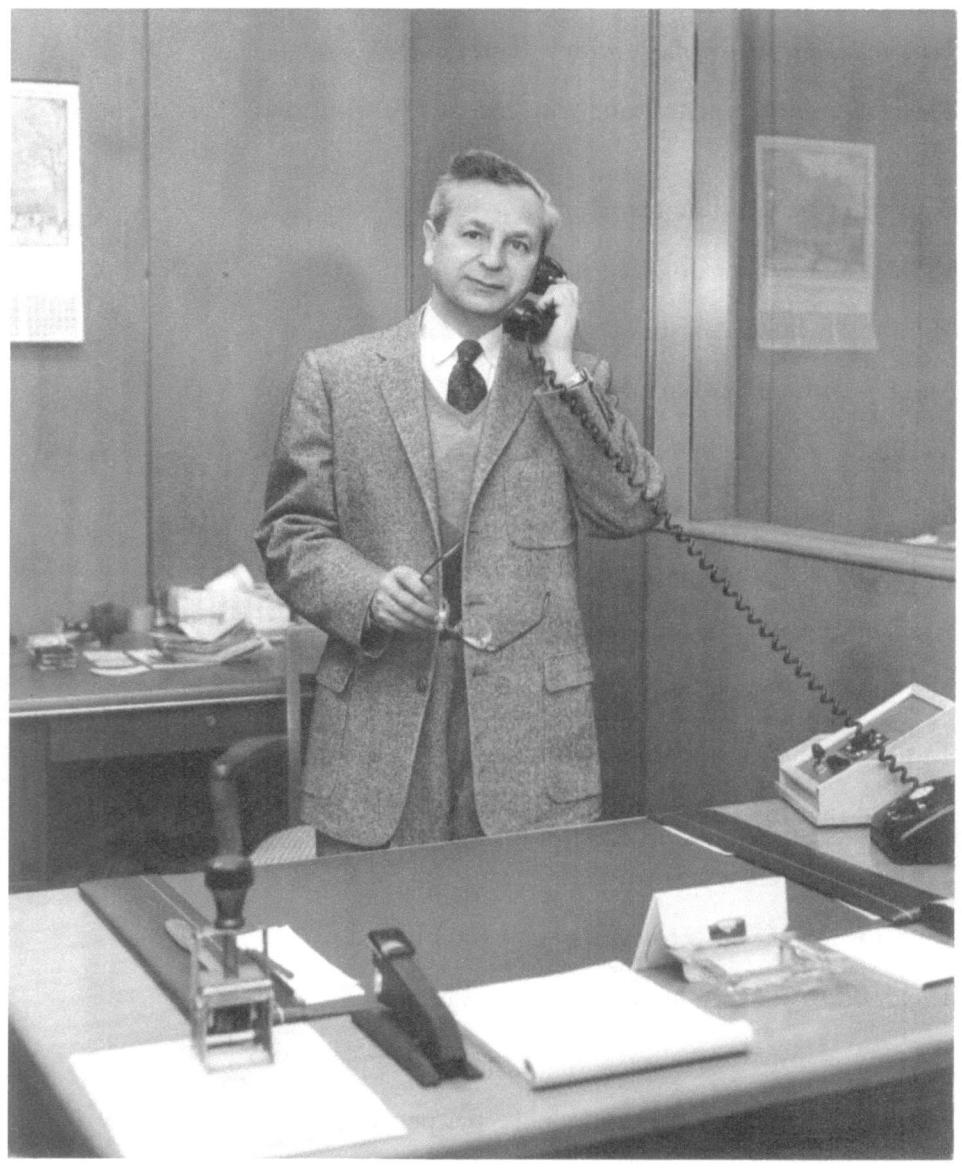

Stage Struck

While I was a student in college

Studying and absorbing all sorts of knowledge

I just happened to take a class in play production.

By that class and that professor I was so stimulated

I succumbed completely to its and his seduction.

And ever since I have had a close affinity for the stage

And to those who play upon it.

Using their talents and their life-long learning

To portray the feelings and emotions

Of the characters they play.

Nowhere else can one enjoy this experience in quite the same way.

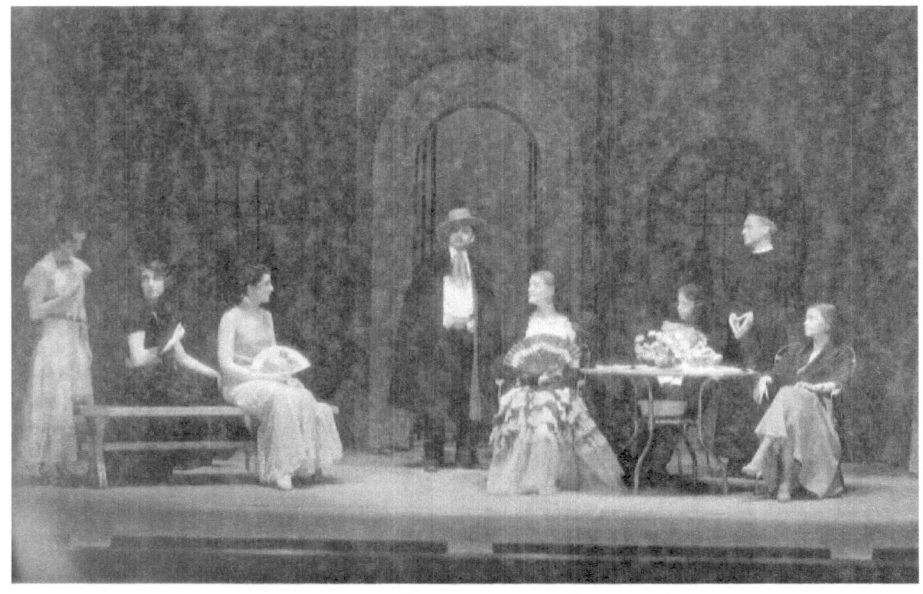

1931 University of Wisconsin Play Production

P. H. Scott

About eighty years ago, when I was a student in college

Where I was working to increase my store of knowledge

I had for one of my classes a man by the name of Preston H. Scott.

This man turned out to be a very good teacher and he taught us a lot.

I found him to be a person of great sincerity and integrity.

In fact, he became my role model from then on.

We became good friends and he was someone I could depend on.

After I got my B.A., Professor Scott procured for me an out state scholarship to the University of Wisconsin

Where I earned an M.A., or Master of Arts degree.

This helped determine the next step in my career

Which was to become a teacher like him for many a year.

Grad School

In 1930-31 I was a student at the University of Wisconsin

Studying for a master's degree.

I was fortunate enough to be on a scholarship

So did not have to pay the outstate fee.

This was in the midst of what became known as the "Great Depression"

Which lasted a long time, session after session.

While there, I lived on fifteen dollars a week

Twelve for room and board and three left over to seek

What little divertissement I could

Like an occasional movie or a snack.

That way for entertainment I managed not to lack.

Also sports events like football and
basketball I was able to attend

With my weekly allowance, my dad
would send.

I enjoyed my stay in Madison,
Wisconsin, very much

And at year's end I received my new
certificate which I loved to touch.

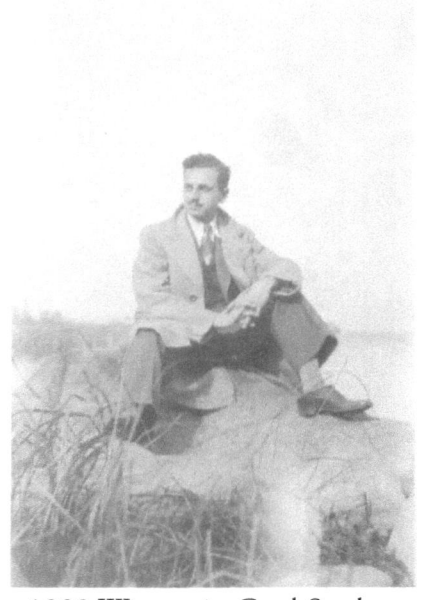

1930 Wisconsin Grad Student

Part VI: Trowbridge

Renaissance

After living for 51 years in our house in Oak Park

Ann and I decided it was time to embark

On a new career and a different life.

So we moved to a senior residence, me and my wife.

Now instead of occasionally venturing forth to meet with others

We daily communicate with everyone, sisters and brothers

As well as parents and grandparents

Who all dwell in one building in separate apartments

But eat together in a community dining room

And so maintain a social relationship

Which is helpful and beneficial to tip

The scales of a rational and reasonable life together.

Trowbridge I

The Park at Trowbridge,

Home of two hundred seniors or more,

Provides food, shelter and entertainment galore.

People who live here are easy to meet

And always each other ready to greet.

A more cohesive community would be hard to find

As residents are happy in both body and mind.

Therefore, if a new home you now seek

And are qualified by age and proper mystique

You need look no further than this

For better living, and repose here you cannot miss.

Breakfast at the Trowbridge

There is a lovely lady named Warren

Whose first name, Lucille, was acquired when she was bor-en.

She sits at the breakfast table with me and some others

Every morning, and the conversation that usually ensues

Is interesting and informative enough to diminish any blues

I think there are few others of her ilk

Her talk and her demeanor are as smooth as silk.

As the time slips away while we all have our say.

Dinnertime at the Trowbridge

At the dinner table each evening we are four

No need actually to have any more.

Adrienne, Sylvia, Ann and I

Ingest our victuals as time goes by.

We discuss the news and events of the day

And betimes one of us will speak up and say

Something that is of interest to all;

Could be an occurrence that happened at the Mall.

The last meal of the day culminates our gastronomic intake,

And it comes to an end with some sort of dessert

Often enough, a generous helping of delicious cake.

Sanctuary

Back in 1915 when I was a lad of eight

I remember thinking what was to be my fate?

When another little boy by the name of Dow

In play one wintry day after school did now

Roughly and angrily push me into an icy pool

After proclaiming loudly and boldly that I "had killed his Lord."

And for that reason I should be made to suffer

And the punishment for my sins could only be rougher.

All my life since I have known what it meant to be a Jew

And different incidents, throughout the years

Have unfortunately proved to confirm my fears.

Therefore, when I came to live at Trowbridge in my declining years

I found that on this score I need have no fears.

For both Jew and non-Jew were treated alike,

And no one would ever be known to utter the word, "kike."

Here "matzo ball" soup is served every Friday night

And Rabbis appear regularly to offer up the light.

"Pork loin" is also offered sometimes at dinner

So everyone to his or her own taste can be a winner.

Thus proving that people with a different religion

Can live in harmony without there being even a smidgen

Of discord or dispute among those of good repute.

Interracial Harmony
(Martin Luther King Day)

The Park at Trowbridge is truly an integrated community

From negative race relations there is complete immunity

Blacks and whites do everything together

There is never a question as to whether

To sit at the same table with each other

Behavior is just like between sister and brother

They play games like Bridge, Backgammon, and Scrabble.

And with all the mirth and babble

Not a single difference is noticeable among the participants.

Trowbridge II

At the Park at Trowbridge, a home for senior residents

Dwell many individuals still of good sense.

In addition to good food and decent lodging

There is entertainment each afternoon and night.

We have musicians, singers, dancers, and more

As part of the variety of programs galore

Also we have current events, poetry reading, play readings and such

Happenings calculated for the occupants to do much.

By all these goodies we are so beguiled

That we are stimulated and bemused and nary an objection is ever filed.

Breakfast at Table 9

Everyone knows the legendary King Arthur and his Knights of the Round Table.

While it may be no more than just an interesting fable

It serves my purpose in order to explain my own round table.

For I too have a round table at which I sit every day

Along with six damsels who rightly enter this play.

They are Adrienne, Blanch, Elaine, Gladys, Lucille, and Minna

Who all meet together for breakfast almost every morning

When all appear promptly without any warning.

We have our oatmeal and chit-chat after the previous night

And get our day started properly with everything all right.

The Park at Trowbridge

My wife, Ann, and I have been living in this senior residence for more than three years

Leaving our homestead and coming here caused no shedding of tears.

For nearly fifty-five years we enjoyed living in Oak Park.

The act of making the move was anything but a merry lark.

Now that we're here we find that there are advantages galore.

We socialize with many of the residents daily, more and more.

Members of the staff have been courteous, attentive and helpful.

Not only is the food here nutritious and plentiful

It is also more than adequate, varied, and deliciously edible.

All in all, we are glad we made this big change,

And hope to continue to enjoy the interesting activities of great range.

Andrea of the Park at Trowbridge

There is a young woman who flits about in our dining room

Who is fleet of foot and quick of wit.

When no one else comes to our table to take our orders

She appears from nowhere or perhaps from her quarters.

As in the story of Jason and the Golden Fleece

Andrea is like a goddess out of ancient Greece.

She is efficient, effective and exciting to watch

And with no apparent effort and even less obvious skill

She accomplishes her objective with a show of good will.

Ida, of the Park of Trowbridge

Ida is the grandmother of six.

Without her we'd be in a pretty bad fix.

For she comes to clean our apartment every week,

And leave it in a condition that is at its very peak.

She does this with such apparent ease and agility

That it would be the envy of anyone with lesser ability.

She is always in good humor, and we like her a lot

Because she does all this whether it is cold or it is hot.

Donna of the Park at Trowbridge

There is a young woman on the staff of this Senior Residence

Who is all things for the people here, ladies and gents.

She is pretty as a picture, smart, and capable too.

She is busy as a bee, and has many things to do.

She is involved in many of the programs that are offered daily,

And goes about her work efficiently and gaily.

Donna is her name, and participation is her game.

She can be found in the "Fitness Room" conducting exercises for the residents.

She has a hand in theatrics with the play-reading group,

And she helps out with the publication, "Live Well" that comes out once a month.

Donna does all these things with aplomb and finesse,

And that is why I like her so much, I must confess.

Claudia of the Park at Trowbridge

Claudia is the manager of the Trowbridge dining room.

We see her every day during the dinner hour.

She sees to it that things run smoothly

and everyone gets taken care of, all within her power.

She flits about the room, darting here and there, filling every void with tender care.

To find someone so devoted to her job, and doing it so well is surely rather rare.

Claudia not only does all this with subtlety and finesse,

She also does it without any apparent effort or any sign of undue stress.

The residents here enjoy her care and attention to detail

And hereby express their appreciation for her good deeds with our fail.

Edith of the Park at Trowbridge

There is a lovely lady residing at The Park at Trowbridge whom I have known for some time now.

Her name is Edith, and she is the most sensitive and caring person that I know.

She will go out of her way to offer solace and comfort to anyone in need.

In some cases to those individuals, that may mean quite a bit.

Indeed, Edith makes me think of one of the goddesses of ancient Greece and Rome,

The one called Athena, who was the goddess of wisdom and benevolence.

Edith often is seen performing such acts

And that is true according to the facts.

She is truly the epitome of all the virtues,

And I think of her as a veritable modern goddess too.

The Round Table Now

Everybody knows about "King Arthur and the Knights of the Round Table."

Well, we have our round table here at the Park at Trowbridge,

And that is not just a fable.

The members of this exalted group might be called the "Knightesses"

Without any one of them being encumbered by light or dark, and lengthy tresses.

Their names are Adrienne, Blanche, Minna, Elaine, Gladys, and Lucille.

Then there has to be someone like King Arthur, to complete the deal.

So that is where I come in, making it all seem very real.

Part VII: Miscellaneous

The Great Depression

Seven long years it lasted,

It was as if a black cloud covered everything.

The banks were closed and business was practically at a standstill.

The years from 1929 to 1936 were years of infamy.

No jobs, no work, everyone was living from hand to mouth.

It was a gloomy world we inhabited.

When would it all end?

But end it did. In 1936 the economy began to improve.

Suddenly there were jobs to be had

Life's momentum once more slowly re-emerged

And the economy once again was functioning.

We who experienced life in the doldrums

Now took heart and once again looked forward to life, love, work and play.

For this was the new millennium we had all long sought.

World War I

In 1918, the United States was forced to join the war that was raging in Europe

Because the German navy was using their submarines to torpedo our ships.

In those days fighting a war on land consisted of firing weapons and lobbing hand grenades

From your trenches into the trenches of the enemy

Across what was known as "No Man's Land," the space between the two lines of trenches.

During cold weather the men in the trenches had difficulty firing their rifles because of freezing hands and fingers.

At that time I was ten years old and in the fifth grade in school.

There we were taught to knit and make what were called "wristlets."

They were woolen hand and forearm coverings which left the fingers free.

They were just what the soldiers needed to keep warm and still be able to shoot.

That was the contribution of the children of America to help win the war.

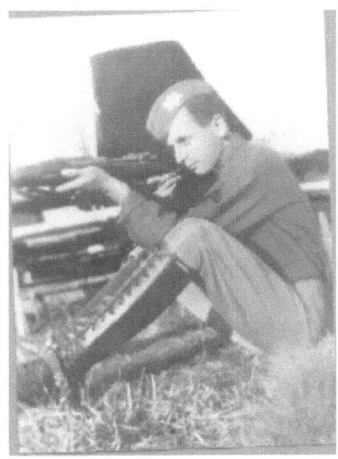

Milton on the Rifle
Range

World War II

In January of 1943, while World War II

Raced overseas in Europe

From the safety of my civilian job by the military draft I was caught up.

First, in training at Camp Wallace, Texas, I would strive

To learn the art of soldiering and how to keep alive.

Then, from basic training I was relieved

And reassigned to clerical school by good fortune indeed.

Because of my record in the Personal File of having been a pedagogue

I was promoted from Private to Corporal

And in the field of military education I became a cog.

Later when the school was closed, I became a company clerk

And then as a sergeant I completed my army work.

The war was over in 1945, and I came home still very much alive.

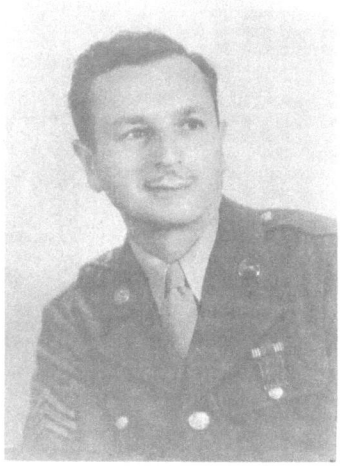

1945 in the US Infantry

Thoughts Macabre (With apologies to Edgar Allan Poe and Dr. Kevorkian, otherwise known as Dr. Death)

When one has reached the age of a hundred years and more

One can't help but wonder what lies in store.

Is there a future for one so old?

Or should one rightly be so bold

As to hope for life on earth to go on

For years on end to grow in wisdom and wit

In spite of a body that is no longer fit

To cope with the vicissitudes of that dastardly deed

To commit and so bring about your own demise!

Or would that be a conclusion not so wise?

Longevity or How to Live a Long Life

To live a long life of a hundred or more

Certain things are required to reach that score.

Ancestors with good genes are important to longevity,

To avoid the pitfalls of a life of mere brevity.

Next, if you are a man, you need a good wife

That in itself does make for a good life.

Then you have to follow the rules of good living

No smoking, no drinking, nothing to excess

Moderation in everything leads to the best

Life you can have here on this earth.

Also, do not forget the importance of laughter and mirth.

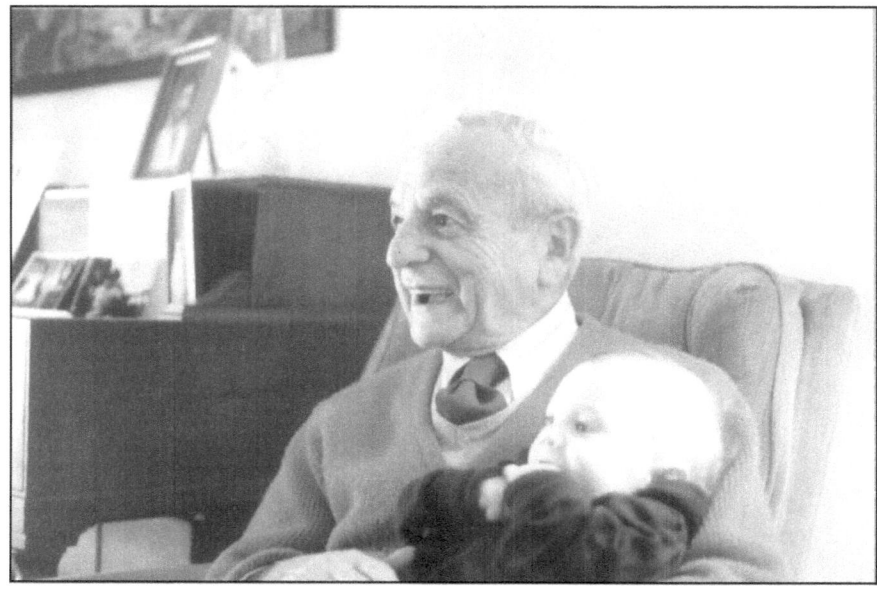

A Reason To Smile

Oldest Jewish Americans Brunch

On May 9, 2008, I attended the annual celebration

Of the 95 and over Jewish Americans

Among the oldest in the nation.

I met others like myself who had lived a long life

Albeit, not always free from worry or strife.

We were welcomed by the staff of Elderlink.

A branch of the Jewish Federation of Metropolitan Detroit

Who in caring for people are very adroit.

We were entertained with song, food, drink, and much more

With good fellowship, social relationships, and colloquy galore.

For which we all were thankful and grateful and now look forward to next year.

The Republican (Hypothetical)

Hillary Clinton and Barack Obama have been battling for a long, long time.

They go to and fro, hither and thither, with little reason and no rhyme.

For all the good it will do them they might as well give up

For John McCain is the man who will win the cup

And he will do it with ease on election day

Making all his valiant efforts right fully pay.

This is the feeling of a staunch Republican

After a long and difficult campaign run.

The Democrat

Hilary Clinton or Barack Obama?

Which one will it be?

Worry, worry, worry, oh woe is me.

One is a woman, the other a black.

We don't like McCain, not only because he's a Republican

But also because he is for the war in Iraq.

We know that Bush did start the war against the foe

But we don't need someone else in office to go with that flo.

Democrats are apparently opposed to the war

Which may very well cause their hopes for victory to soar.

The Agnostic

Much has been written and said about life after death

For centuries, poets and pundits have struggled to define heaven and hell.

We still look up to the sky when for beneficence we pray

And down into "Hades" where evil is punished all the way.

By definition, the immortal soul cannot die

So where does it go for the future to lie?

There are those who think that in to other humans they are transposed.

While some believe that into the bodies of animals they are disposed.

In my own case, I do not hold with either of these views.

In part because a long time ago when I was a mere slip of a lad

I suffered from something that was not really so bad.

It was a case of what is known as syncope

Or infrequent spells of fainting, and that was happening to me.

As a result, I found that each time I became unconscious

I had an out of life feeling of vacuity

Or a sense of nonentity and finality.

Disenchantment

My distaste for religion began when I was very young.

Hebrew I was supposed to learn with the prayers coming trippingly off my tongue.

I have never forgotten from the time I was seven

Studying the language of my ancestors 'til I was eleven.

Every afternoon after school with what I thought was a dirty old man

Who was supposed to inculcate in me the knowledge of Hebrew

So that when in the synagogue the chanting began, I could do it too.

However, the time I spent on wintry afternoons in this occupation

Meant I could not be where I wanted at another location.

Sledding down "Upson Hill" with my friends

For which I felt there could be no amends.

Another reason for my disenchantment

Was that I never was told the meaning of a single word

So I never understood what I was being taught was all about

And that left me with the feeling that I was nothing more than a lout.

Etiology and Biology
Or Cause and Effect

Recently, my right leg has been bothering me

With pain in my thigh and numbness below the knee.

To Dr. Barry Feldman, I did go to find out the cause.

After an examination and X-rays a diagnosis appeared without pause.

What I have is called "lumbar spinal stenosis"

Owing to a degree of scoliosis.

Which means in plain English, blockage of a nerve in the spine.

This was my problem and it was all mine.

Now that I know all about the etiology

I realize it is simply a matter of physiology!

Monotheism

Throughout the ages, man has sought for a source of spiritual guidance especially in times of stress.

There has always been a need for moral support by human beings of something or someone outside themselves

To provide comfort, hope, and solace that is beyond their capability.

Over the course of time, this source has taken various forms

All of which are a distinct departure from the usual norms.

At one time it was an animal, at another a wooden idol.

Among the ancient Greeks, Norse, and Romans to fulfill this need

There arose a veritable school of benefactors.

These creations were known as Gods and Goddesses.

Some of them were Apollo, the sun God, Thor, the God of thunder, and Poseidon, the God of the Sea.

Then there was Athena, the Goddess of war, Diana, the Goddess of the hunt, and Juno, the Goddess of Wisdom.

It took some time, but eventually an ideal emerged.

That is what we have now, one meritorious, omnipotent, single deity, one God for all.

Daedalus and Icarus, Father and Son

A long time ago, there was a man who wanted to fly like a bird.

The story about him is one that you very likely have already heard.

His name, as I remember was Daedalus.

In this respect he was very different from the rest of us.

With the aid of his son, Icarus, he fashioned a pair of wings,

And then he tested them for durability and safety.

They worked so well he thought he could trust them greatly.

Unfortunately, as the story goes, the boy flew too close to the sun

And it melted the wax on the wings.

So down he fell with all of his things.

Much later on, a real airplane was built by two brothers, Orville and Wilber
Wright

Who worked on it assiduously until they got it just right.

It was a bi-plane, with two wings and a single propeller

With a seat for the pilot and an engine built in their bicycle shop.

Now the airplane has developed through the ensuing years

And people fly everywhere and every day,

Doing it presumably with out any more fears.

Shakespeare's "Hamlet" Revisited

Now that I have passed the century mark and added two years more

I often find myself reminiscing about the days of yore.

One of the things I recall from the distant past

Is a course in Shakespeare that did for me truly last.

I remember particularly Hamlet's famous soliloquy

In which he utters these words in an outburst of obloquy:

"To be or not to be: that is the question:

Whether 'tis nobler in the mind to suffer

The slings and arrows of outrageous fortune,

Or to take arms against a sea of troubles,

And by opposing end them?"

What Hamlet is saying is that it might be better "to slough off this mortal coil and leave this vale of tears and toil."

This drastic choice may sound too morbid for some

But that is what happens when the time has come.

Jonathan Swift and the Fantastic Sea Voyage

It was circa 1727 when an English author by the name of Jonathan Swift

Wrote some stories for which he seemed to have a great gift.

One of these stories was called "Gulliver's Travels,"

A part of which would have been suitable for many riding saddles.

In this book, Swift tells of Gulliver's visits to many different lands

Where he finds the inhabitants to be of curiously different brands.

Among them were the little people of a county called Lilliput,

Where everything and everybody were "little' as measured by the foot.

These people were called Lilliputians, and they were really small,

So whatever hazards they faced, they did not have far to fall.

Then there were the Brobdingnagians, giants with everything to match,

No matter how large an object thrown to them, it was easy for them to catch.

Perhaps the most unusual place that Gulliver found was the country of the Huchinyans

Where the people were all horses

And their language had a peculiarly strange sound.

My Good Samaritan

My Wife, Ann, in age is ninety-five

But she is still able to do much to help keep me alive.

She has assisted me in all my transactions,

And also in many other necessary functions.

Since I am now one hundred and two

There are many things I no longer can do.

Telephone calls, letter writing, and business activities

Are now beyond the realm of my capabilities.

Fortunately, Ann is still able to handle these matters.

Without her aid and assistance I don't know what I would do.

She is my Good Samaritan in many projects whether old or new.

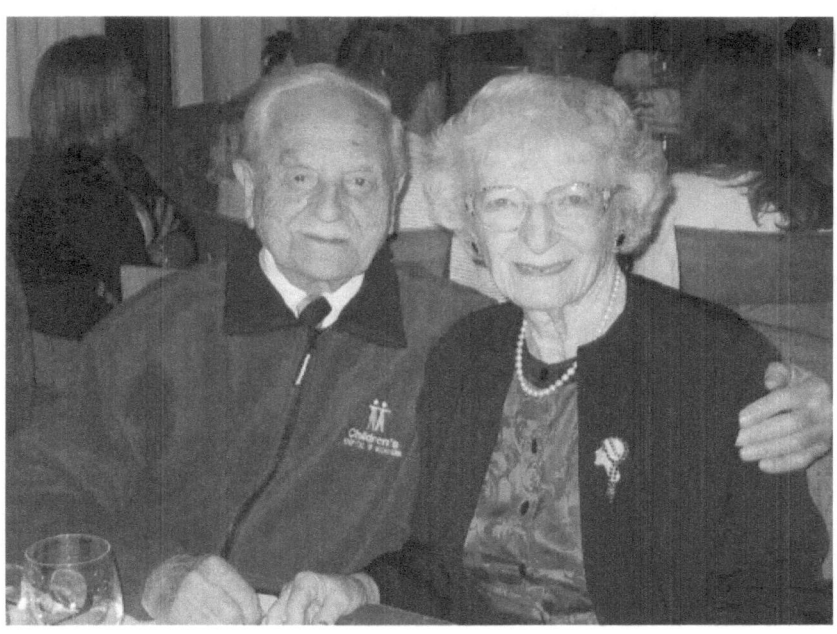

POSTSCRIPT

It is my hope that to the occasional reader, this work will have some of the joy and satisfaction it brought to its creator.

About the Author

Milton J. Ross was born Max Rosenberg on September 9, 1907 in New Britain, Connecticut. His sisters called him Milton as they preferred that to Max and the name stuck. After retirement, he obtained a copy of his birth certificate to apply for a passport and discovered two things when the certificate arrived. First his birthday, which he had always celebrated on the 6th of September was actually the 9th, making him 3 days younger, and second that his first name was actually Max. When he had shortened the name to Ross, he changed it legally from "Milton Rosenberg" to "Milton Ross," so between that misnomer and the wrong birth date he may not really exist (legally anyway).

The fact that he does very much exist is documented by these poems which he has penned over the last 2 years. They cover a wide range of topics and eras and give the meaning of this remarkable man. His careers included a highly successful high school teacher of English Literature and Director of High School Plays. He still has adoring former students who visit frequently and are now in their 80s themselves. He served in the Army's Infantry Corp during World War II and then became the treasurer of a wholesale corporation from 1948 until retirement in 1976. Milton next began volunteer tax work for the elderly for twenty three years and by the end of that stint, most of his clients were younger than he was. Starting around the time of his 100th birthday, Milton took up a new hobby of writing poetry, and this book is the result.

Milton loves to tell people that he has a Unitarian Family" consisting of: 1 wife, 1 son, 1 daughter-in-law, 1 grandson, and 1 Dog (belonging to son and grandson). It is for these people and the many loving friends and family members that he publishes this book for all to enjoy.

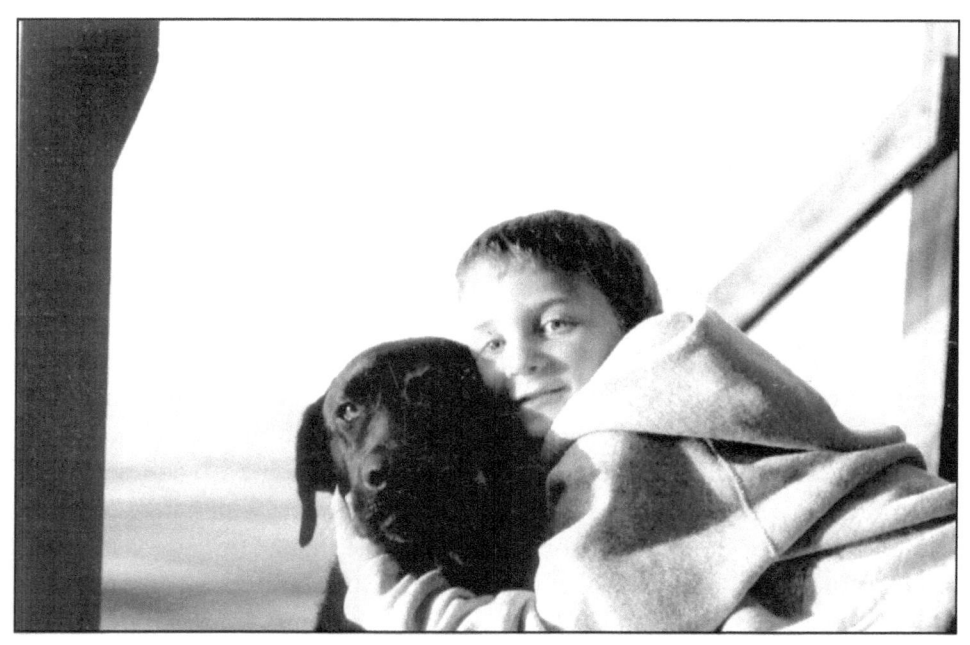

Grandson Peter and puppy